This

LUTHERAN BOOK OF PRAYER

is presented to

_____

_____

by

_____

_____

Lutheran

BOOK *of* PRAYER

CONCORDIA PUBLISHING HOUSE

Saint Louis

SEVENTEENTH PRINTING

PRINTED IN THE UNITED STATES OF AMERICA

The book also contains Psalms, to draw attention to the prayer book of the Holy Scriptures
with which every Christian soul should be familiar.

PREFACE

✠

THIS book is issued in the conviction that
the prayer of a Christian is not a futile gesture
or a mere pious exercise, but a mighty means
by which he obtains help and strength in his
various needs. The words of promise: "Call
upon Me in the day of trouble; I will deliver
thee, and thou shalt glorify Me," Ps. 50:15, are
one of the foundation stones on which this work
is based.

Needless to say, this collection of prayers is
not published with the design of curtailing the
praises and petitions which the Christian, with
the promptings of the Holy Spirit, formulates
himself when he appears before God. It is in-
tended rather to stimulate and aid such praying
and to assist the believer in making his whole
life one of communion with our Father in
heaven. Many Christians, meditating on the
situation in which they, either singly or together
with their fellow men, are placed, desire to
have some thoughts, words, and phrases sug-
gested in which their inmost longing can become definite and articulate. To meet such
desire these prayers are offered.

The book also contains Psalms, to draw attention to the prayer book of the Holy Scriptures, with which every child of God should be familiar.

The Publishers hope that all those who use the *Book of Prayer* will find fulfilled for themselves the Savior's gracious promises: "Ask, and it shall be given you; seek, and ye shall find; knock, and it shall be opened unto you." Matt. 7:7.

The Lord's Prayer

✠

OUR Father who art in heaven.
Hallowed be Thy name.
Thy kingdom come.
Thy will be done on earth as it is in heaven.
Give us this day our daily bread.
And forgive us our trespasses, as we forgive those
who trespass against us.
And lead us not into temptation,
but deliver us from evil.
For Thine is the kingdom
and the power
and the glory
forever and ever.

AMEN

Prayers

FOR MORNINGS AND EVENINGS

Sunday

✠

Lord God, Thou art the High and Lofty One who inhabitest eternity; Thy name is Holy. Yet Thou hast promised to dwell with him who is of a contrite and humble spirit. I pray Thee on this first day of the week to let all who hear Thy holy Word experience the fulfillment of this promise. Through Thy holy Gospel enter Thou into our hearts and make us dwelling places of Thy grace. As Thy Word is proclaimed this day, let me receive it with a believing heart and be a doer of Thy Word, and not a hearer only. Restore to me the joy of Thy salvation, and give me strength to put into practice what I have heard. Keep me a humble learner as long as I dwell on earth, and at last receive me, as Thy child and heir, into Thy heavenly habitations; through Jesus Christ, Thy Son, our Redeemer. Amen.

Sunday

✠

I THANK Thee, O Father, Lord of heaven and earth, that Thou hast again revealed to me Thy grace and forgiveness in Christ Jesus by the preaching of Thy holy Gospel. Bless Thy Word wherever it has been proclaimed this day, and let it be a power unto salvation to all who have heard it. Open the eyes of those who are still too blind to know Thee, the only true God, and Jesus Christ, whom Thou hast sent. Send out Thy light and Thy truth to all who are without Christ, without God, without hope, in the world, and lead them to the knowledge of Thy glory in the face of Jesus Christ, our Lord. Forgive my sins for the sake of my Redeemer. Let Thy Word be my constant comfort in life and death. Let it guide me wherever I go, cheer me as I prepare for sleep, talk to me when I arise, that, whether I live, I live unto Thee, and whether I die, I die unto Thee. In life and death I am Thine own, through Christ, our Redeemer. Amen.

Monday

MORNING

✠

LORD, in this morning hour I come boldly to Thy throne of grace in full assurance that I shall obtain mercy and find grace this day and help in time of trouble. I need Thy guidance and grace as I return to my daily task. Grant me true faithfulness in the performance of my calling. Guard me against selfishness and carelessness. In the pursuance of my daily work may I do my duty not with eyeservice as a manpleaser, but as a servant of Christ, doing the will of God from the heart. Grant useful employment to all who are out of work. Feed me with food convenient for me, and teach me to receive my daily bread with thanksgiving. Grant me that godliness and contentment without which there can be no true happiness, and let me so walk in this temporal world that I lose not the things eternal. For Jesus' sake. Amen.

Monday

✠

O LORD, Thou hast searched me and known me. Thou knowest my downsitting and mine uprising; Thou understandest my thought afar off. Thou compassest my path and my lying down and art acquainted with all my ways. Alas, Thou knowest also how often I have sinned against Thee this very day, how often I have transgressed Thy holy Law, how often I have failed to keep my promises of loyalty to Thee and Thy Word. Lord, do not enter into judgment with Thy servant. Deal not with me after my sins, and reward me not according to my iniquities; but graciously blot out all my trespasses for the sake of Thine own Son, in whom I have redemption through His blood, even the forgiveness of my sins. As the night comes upon me, I again flee to Thee for Thy gracious protection, firmly trusting that Thou wilt keep Thy children safe against all dangers and evils of body and soul. Grant to me and all Thy children refreshing sleep, that tomorrow I may serve Thee with renewed strength in my daily calling. In Jesus' name I ask it. Amen.

Tuesday

✠

Gracious Lord, who hast promised to be with us alway, I ask Thee to dwell in our home and hearts and bless us with Thy peace. Keep us all in the saving faith, which is in Jesus Christ as our Lord and Redeemer. Give to us the grace and the desire to walk with Thee in Christian love. Preserve in our home the fruits of Thy Holy Spirit, contentment, joy, and peace. Remove from our hearts envy, strife, contention. Forgive us all our sins, each and every one. Forgiven by Thee, make us forgiving and thoughtful. Let not the duties and tasks of the day make us dissatisfied and peevish. And, Lord, I ask Thee to bless all the homes of the nations with peace. Wherever there are misunderstandings, ill will, strife, quarrels, let Thy Word enter in and reconcile those who have been estranged from one another and from Thee. Grant that prodigal sons and erring daughters may return with penitent hearts. Let Thy Word dwell in our household richly, that we may live in peace with Thee and one another and find our greatest joy in Jesus Christ, our Lord and Redeemer. Amen.

Tuesday

✠

I THANK Thee, almighty Ruler of heaven and earth, that Thou hast preserved me from sickness and misfortune, from dishonor and shame, from famine and want, from hunger and thirst. Thou hast given to me food according to my needs. Thou hast granted me life and favor, and Thy presence has preserved my spirit. Oh, give thanks unto the Lord; for He is good, for his mercy endureth forever. Lord, in this evening hour I come to Thee, acknowledging my manifold transgressions of the day. I am ashamed of myself and blush as I lift up my face to Thee, O God. Yet, trusting in the atoning sacrifice of Thy Son, I ask Thee graciously to forgive me all my sins and to cover them with the righteousness of Jesus, my Savior, that, though they be as scarlet, they shall be as white as snow. I come to Thee, seeking Thy continued protection this night and all the days of my life, until I stand in Thy presence, where there is no night, but everlasting day and glory. Hear me for the sake of my heavenly Redeemer. Amen.

Wednesday

✠

LORD Jesus, Thou hast chosen me out of the world to be Thine own in time and eternity. Though I am no longer of the world, Thou hast not as yet taken me out of this pilgrimage to my eternal home. I am still in this world, surrounded by innumerable dangers and constantly exposed to many temptations. Let me never forget that the world passeth away and the lust thereof and that only he that doeth the will of God abideth forever. Increase and preserve in me that faith in Thee and Thy redeeming work which is the victory that overcometh the world. Give me a more fervent love to Thee, never choosing the things of this world — its riches, its glories, its pleasures — and forgetting Thee and Thy salvation. Teach me to rise above the world's mockery, hatred, and threats, knowing that, even if I should be deprived of some temporal advantage, the world can never rob me of Thy grace and fatherly care. Keep me as a child of Thy household on the narrow way of life, and receive me at last into Thy heavenly home. Amen.

Wednesday
EVENING

✠

LORD of hosts, I thank Thee for the many blessings which Thou hast granted us as citizens of our country. I acknowledge that we are not worthy of any of Thy manifold mercies. I, as well as we, our Church and our country, have sinned against Thee. I have been ungrateful, and have deserved Thy judgments rather than the privileges so often and so shamefully abused. Remember, I ask Thee, Thy mercies of old, and for the sake of Thine only-begotten Son, our Redeemer, forgive us our guilt. Guard our country from war and bloodshed, from revolution and civic strife, from famine and pestilence. Preserve to us and to our children the liberty and the peace we have enjoyed, and let no enemy from within or without succeed in depriving our nation of these treasures of Thy mercy. Grant the rulers of our country, our state, and our community, wisdom and courage to uphold righteousness, that under this government we may lead a quiet and peaceful life in all godliness and honesty. And may Thy church flourish to Thy glory and the salvation of souls redeemed by Thy Son, our Lord. Amen.

Thursday

✠

LORD Jesus, by Thy regenerating grace I am reborn and have become a new creature through faith in Thy redeeming blood. Yet I confess to Thee, Searcher of hearts, that in me also, that is, in my flesh, dwelleth no good thing. Evil thoughts, wicked desires, and sinful passions constantly arise within me; they oppose my sincerest efforts to do Thy will and burden my conscience with guilt and shame. I come to Thee in this morning hour, confessing my own weakness and asking Thee for the sake of Thy suffering and death to forgive and blot out my shortcomings and help me in my daily struggle against the evil desires of my sinful nature. Direct my thoughts and actions to do Thy will. Lovingly strengthen me to put off daily the old man with all evil desires and put on the new man, created after God in righteousness and true holiness. Make me daily purer in my desires, cleaner in speech, holier in actions, that I may be blameless and harmless, with the sons of God, shining as a light in the world of sin until Thou callest me home to that perfect glory of eternal life. Amen.

Thursday

EVENING

✠

OUR help, O Lord, cometh from Thee, who hast made heaven and earth. Thou hast been my Refuge and Strength during this day, a very present Help in every trouble. Thou hast given Thine angels charge over me to keep me in all my ways. As the night approaches, I know that Thou art my Fortress, my God, in whom I will trust. As I lie down to rest, Thou who keepest me shalt neither slumber nor sleep. Let Thine eyes ever be open and Thy protecting hands spread over my home and those of my fellow men. Give to the sick a restful, refreshing sleep and to all who are sorrowful the consolation of Thy gracious presence. Our time, our life, our salvation, O mighty and merciful God, are in Thy hands. If my last hour shall come this night, abide with me and preserve me in true faith. I know in whom I have believed: in Thee, my Father, and in my Lord Jesus Christ, who died for me. To Thee I commit my body and soul for safekeeping in time and eternity. In Jesus' name. Amen.

Friday

✠

O LAMB of God, which takest away the sin of the world, on this memorial day of Thy death I give Thee thanks that Thou hast redeemed me lost and condemned creature, purchased and won me from all sins, from death, and from the power of the devil, to be Thine own in time and eternity. Create in me that true thankfulness which will never forget Thy love wherewith Thou hast loved us and which has caused Thee to give Thyself into death for us and our salvation. Give me that boldness and never-failing courage of faith which cannot but speak the things I have seen and heard. Open Thou my lips that, out of the abundance of a heart which knows Thee, I may speak to others of Thy matchless love. Make me an ambassador for Thee, my Savior, Thy personal messenger to my fellow men. Give me a heart willing to support the work of missions carried on by Thy church and to sacrifice gladly of my time and money, that in every country, city, hamlet, throughout the world Thy praises be sung as the Lamb that was slain and has redeemed us to God by His blood. Amen.

Friday

✠

I WILL both lay me down in peace and sleep, for Thou, Lord, only makest me dwell in safety. Thou everlasting Rock of Ages, in whom is unfailing strength, wilt keep us all in perfect peace whose mind is stayed on Thee. Thou, O Father, art able to do exceeding abundantly above all that we ask and think. Thou hast promised us that all things work together for good to them that love Thee. Why should any worry and sorrow disturb me and rob me of my peace? Thou, O Savior, hast taken away all my guilt, washed me clean from all my sin, and blotted out all my iniquities by Thy blood. Thou art my Light and my Salvation; whom shall I fear? Thou, O Holy Spirit, having begun a good work, wilt perform it until the Day of Jesus Christ. Thou art the Strength of my life; of whom shall I be afraid? To Thee, O Triune God, I commend myself, my loved ones, all mankind. Under the shadow of Thy wings I will lie down and sleep, for Thou, Lord, surely wilt make me dwell in safety. I say this confidently in the name of Jesus. Amen.

Saturday

✠

I LAID me down and slept; I waked; for the Lord has sustained me. Protected by Thy mighty hand, I have passed safely through the night. Lord, I am not worthy of the least of all the mercies which Thou hast shown to Thy servant. I thank Thee for Thy gracious protection. As I think of all those who are in sorrow and tribulation, in sickness and pain, in poverty or shame, in anguish of soul, I beseech Thee, the Father of our Lord Jesus Christ, the Father of mercies, and the God of all comfort, that Thou wouldst comfort them with the assurance of Thy unchanging grace and loving-kindness. Strengthen their faith. Preserve them from misbelief, despair, and other great shame and vice. Teach them to humble themselves under Thy mighty hand, recognizing Thy gracious purpose to work through tribulation patience, through patience experience, through experience hope that will not make them ashamed. Help all sufferers to bear their trials until Thine hour of deliverance has come. Set me free from every evil work, and preserve me to Thy heavenly kingdom. In the name of Jesus. Amen.

Saturday

✠

Another week of my life has passed, O Lord. As I look back, how swiftly have the days, the hours gone by! Behold, Thou hast made my days as a handbreadth. Therefore, Lord, make me to know my end and the measure of my days, what it is, that I may know how frail I am. I poor dying mortal come to Thee, O eternal Lord, who hast been my Dwelling Place in all generations. Thou art the same; and as Thy years shall have no end, so Thou shalt ever remain the Lord, the Lord God, merciful and gracious, long-suffering, and abundant in goodness and truth, keeping mercy for thousands, forgiving iniquity and transgression and sin. To Thee I come in this evening hour. I thank Thee that during the past week Thy compassion did not fail and Thy mercies were new every morning. Thou hast kept me in Thy Word and grace. Shield me with Thy mercy during the coming night that I may go tomorrow with the multitudes to Thy house and with the voice of thanksgiving publish Thy loving-kindness and tell of all Thy wondrous works; for Jesus' sake. Amen.

Sunday

MORNING

✠

HEAVENLY Father, who on this first of days didst call forth light out of darkness, shine into my soul with the power of Thy love, and give me a new heart, and create a clean spirit within me. Enlighten also my heart through Thy Gospel to know Thee. Glorious Savior, on this day Thou didst rise from the tomb and prove Thyself the Redeemer of all the world; give me faith to accept Thee wholly for the forgiveness of all my sin, and grant me grace to rise to newness of life. Holy Spirit, who on this day didst charge the Church with joyous faith and vigor, fill me also with Thy healing, Thy gift to speak, Thy strength to love. O Holy Trinity, my glorious God, my Strength and Shield, hallow my heart to Thy service this day, give to my worship sincerity and earnestness, and joy to my praise; grant that my fellow believers and I be kept at all time in the unity of faith, and refresh me with Thy Word. In Jesus' name. Amen.

Sunday

✠

LORD God, I thank Thee for the peace of this day, the peace proclaimed to me by Thy Gospel, the peace from the strife and toil of daily tasks, the peace of coming to Thee in prayer. I pray Thee, dear God, let not this peace vanish from my heart and depart from my life. Let not the cares of this world or its joy stifle the seedling of the Word which Thou hast implanted in me. Let not the image of my Savior be defaced in me by doubt and sin, by waywardness or shame. Grant that the joy of worship may be steady and strong within me, even in the days when I may not be able to go to church with my fellow Christians. Grant that the sureness of Thy peace may persist in my heart when the blasts of doubt and evil assail me. Give me refreshing rest this night, and fit me, body and soul, for the labors of this coming week. For Jesus' sake. Amen.

Monday

✠

I THANK Thee, heavenly Father, for the gift of rest and refreshment of body and soul which Thou hast granted me in my worship of yesterday and my slumbers of the night. I pray Thee, make me ready to bend restored energies to the tasks which lie before me. Forgive me all my sins for Jesus' sake, and purge from my heart all selfish desires and purposes which would wrongly use my gifts and powers. Grant that I may day by day put forth efforts which are pleasing to Thee, helpful to my fellow men, and sufficient to provide for my daily needs. Keep me mindful that my service must be done not merely to men, but to Thee. Help me to remember that in all things my sufficiency is of Thee and that whatever I do is to be done to Thy glory. Give me joy in my labor, sincerity in my service, and unselfishness in all my striving. Help me to be faithful in all things, for the sake of Him who died for me. Amen.

Monday

EVENING

✠

DEAR Savior, as I prepare for this night's rest, remind me again that Thou art with me. Thou hast witnessed my life this day, even the thoughts of my heart; O Savior, for the sake of Thy precious blood blot out all my sins. Let them be accounted to Thy charge and not to mine. Cleanse my conscience from all evil, and assure me of the fullness of my peace with God through Thee. Richly endow me with Thy Spirit that I may not waver in my faith in Thee or doubt the reality of Thy presence. Preserve me from fretful care, and let me not falter in my walk with Thee. Fill Thou me with joy in following Thee, and prove to me that Thou dost rule my world and life to my good. Protect and be with all my dear ones; defend my home, my community, my country. Keep from me and all men violence and discord, war and crime, and do Thou by Thy Word stem the tide of sin, and bring forgiveness and love into the world. Be Thou my Rest, my Peace, my All. Amen.

Tuesday

✠

Again, O heavenly Father, Thou dost grant me strength to rise to the tasks of the day. I thank Thee for this Thy mercy and love. Without Thy power upholding me I should be unable to live. Give me a spirit of gratitude for all Thy gifts. Above all, dear Father, keep me grateful for the gift of the forgiveness of all my sins through the merits of Jesus Christ, Thy Son and my Savior. Grant that whatever need, whatever sorrow may beset my day, my faith in this forgiveness may remain steadfast and firm. Let no grief or pain, no doubt or gloom, come between me and the certainty of Thy love. If it is Thy purpose to try me this day with difficulties for the body or the heart, grant that I may by Thy Spirit conquer in this trial and hold fast to Thy mercy, knowing that the sufferings of this time are not worthy to be compared with the glory Thou hast in store for me. Make Thy Word my joy, Thy counsel my guide, Thy presence my peace. In Jesus' name. Amen.

Tuesday

✠

DEAR Father in heaven, as I look this evening upon the hours of the day just past, I am aware of the many ways in which I have offended Thee in word and deed and of the many opportunities for service and love in which I have failed. Forgive me these trespasses and shortcomings for Jesus' sake. Particularly am I mindful of the ways in which I have failed to testify of Thy glorious name and to witness to Thy love to men in Christ Jesus. Give me grace, heavenly Father, to overcome this lack of love, this slowness to confess Thee, this sluggishness in winning souls. Make Thy Christians everywhere zealous to work while it is day in leading others into Thy kingdom. Protect all in their Christian profession, all pastors and teachers, missionaries and Gospel workers. Preserve peace among men that Thy Gospel may run swiftly. If Thou wouldst tonight make an end of my earthly journey, take me to Thee; and if I am to rise to Thy service, fit me more fully. Hear me for the sake of Thy Son, our divine Redeemer. Amen.

Wednesday

✠

Lord God, Thou hast given me another day, a day to live in Thy service and for the good of my fellow men. I am indeed a poor tool in Thy hand and deserving to be cast aside. Forgive me all my sins for Jesus' sake, and by Thy Spirit grant me the fitness to work for Thee this day. I beseech Thee to make me mindful, dear Lord, that I am but a stranger and a pilgrim in this present world. Let me not devote my efforts today to purposes unworthy of Thee; let me not gather treasures merely for this world; let me not serve Mammon. This life is but a vain show; let me not search for an abiding city here. But, Lord, fasten my heart and hope on the life that is in Thee, and let my strivings and desires be directed to the treasures of Thy love. As long as I am in the land of my pilgrimage, hold Thou my hand; keep me from every straying path. If I should stumble in sinful weakness, grant me repentance and faith. For Jesus' sake. Amen.

Wednesday

✠

DEAR Savior, Thou hast brought me safely to the end of this day. I knew not Thy plan for me — what woes, what joys, would today be my lot; and now the day is done. Lord, grant that I may view all things which Thou didst provide for me as meant for my good. Let me view my successes as encouragements and as undeserved gifts coming from Thy gracious hands. Let me regard my perplexities and pains as reminders, chastenings, and directions toward repentance and improvement. The day has gone, O Savior, and I am closer to the hour when I shall see Thee face to face. Let this passing of time make me more ready and watchful for the hour when Thou comest. Let me eagerly prepare myself for Thy Day. O Lord, it is better to depart and be with Thee; wash me in Thy blood that I can stand before Thee. But if Thou wouldst keep me here, then let me be steadfast in faith, abundant in service, warm in love, and unceasing in prayer. Thou hast redeemed me, great God and my Savior; I am Thine. Amen.

Thursday

✠

THE day has dawned, O Father in heaven; and everywhere Thy children are lifting holy hands to Thee for strength for the day and cheer on the road. Let my prayers be acceptable to Thee for the sake of Jesus Christ, my Savior, through whose merits my peace has been made with Thee. Let the Daystar rise in my heart, O Lord, by faith in that Savior through whom my place with Thee is sure forevermore. I beseech Thee, let not only my prayer but my whole life, my every act, thought, and word, be a sacrifice to Thee today, unblamable and worthy, through the power of Thy Spirit. Let the message of Thy Word fill me with the assurance of the forgiveness of my sin; let the counsel of Thy revealed will point out to me the way I am to go; let Thy Spirit give me courage and strength to choose the good part every hour. Hold me in oneness of faith with my fellow Christians, and let me be a salt that has not lost its saltness. Keep me Thine for the sake of Thy Son, my Redeemer. Amen.

Thursday

✠

DEAR Savior, Thou hast purchased me
with Thy blood that I may live in Thy kingdom
and be an heir of life eternal. Thou hast seized
me that I may ever more perfectly lay hold upon
that newness of life wherewith I am to serve
Thee. Again I have been given a day in which
to pursue the prize of this high calling. Where
I have faltered on the road or grown weary in
the search, O Lord, forgive me for the sake of
Thine infinite compassion. Thou knowest the
weakness of my heart, O Christ, and wilt not
reject my plea for mercy. Give me, according
to Thy good pleasure, rest from the rigors of my
toil this day. Renew me also from the weariness
of sin. Let Thy Word nourish me, the Water
of Life refresh my parched soul, and let me become more joyful, more complete, in the quest
for this holiness. Grant that my prayers come
before Thee with more persistence and greater
faith and that my whole life be hid in Thee with
God. I trust in Thee; Thou wilt never forsake
me. Amen.

Friday

✠

SEND me, O Lord, into the tasks of this day with a rejoicing heart. Teach me to labor diligently, to eat and drink to Thy glory, and to think and plan to the ends which Thou hast laid out before me. That I may be truly fitted for the day, remind me again of the mighty work of my Savior Jesus Christ, who redeemed me for Thee, and in whom my sin is forgiven and my place with Thee forever assured. Strengthen in me the sense of that mighty sacrifice of Thy love, that I, too, may become willing to sacrifice for others. Teach me to look upon my life today as a trust given me to help my fellow men. Let me see in my daily tasks, in the need of those who depend on me, in the want and struggle of the world about me, my field for loving service. Impress upon my heart this day that my life, my speech, my faith, is nothing without love. Grant that I be ready to forgive, earnest in my rejoicing with those who are happy, quick in sympathy, and zealous in bearing the burdens of my fellow men. In Jesus' name. Amen.

Friday

EVENING

✠

HEAVENLY Father, I am Thy child. Through Word and Sacrament I have been born anew to Thee. By Jesus' blood and sacrifice I have been received and adopted into Thy family. Dear God, I admit that I have not lived every moment of this day as it becomes a child of Thine. There were times when I strayed, and self-will, negligence, lovelessness, impurity, found a resting place in my heart. I confess these sins to Thee. O Lord, I am not worthy that I should be called Thy child. But I beseech Thee, in fatherly mercy and for the sake of Jesus' blood forgive me my transgressions. Let my faith in this forgiveness be unwavering and sure. Let my gratitude to Thee be expressed in truth and in deed. Without Thy peace, O Father, I am sore at heart and lost; but with the joy of forgiveness I have all things. Comfort me in this Thy forgiving love, and preserve me steadfast in this faith now and forevermore. Amen.

Saturday

✠

I THANK Thee, heavenly Father, for Thine angel guard about my slumbers during the night past and for the day of grace and service into which Thou hast awakened me. Keep me steadfast in the sense of Thy protection and in faith in the redemptive work of Jesus Christ, Thy Son. Lord, make me mindful of the temptations of sinful care, sluggish selfishness, and impure desires, which beset me on every side and from within. Help me in this hour to put on anew the armor of light, that I may be fitted with every weapon of offense and defense against the perils that threaten my spiritual life. Let Thy Gospel call me with new sweetness to be reconciled to Thee; let Thy Spirit call me with new power to follow Thee. Teach me to live this day as though it were my last on earth, knowing that, whether we live or whether we die, we are present with Thee. Be Thou my Protector, my Guide, my Father, for Jesus' sake. Amen.

Saturday

EVENING

✠

ONCE more I would bring to Thee, heavenly Father, the load of a week's sins and shortcomings; and I pray Thee, for the sake of the limitless merit of Christ Jesus, bury its guilt and punishment deep in His wounds. Thou didst in mercy grant me rich opportunities to work in Thy vineyard; but I have come short of that unselfish love which Thy Law demands. I praise and thank Thee, heavenly Father, that my salvation rests altogether on Thy grace and mercy and not on my own efforts and achievements. I pray Thee, let the message of the Gospel and the power of the Sacrament increase my faith. As Thou wilt grant me opportunity to worship Thee in Thy sanctuary tomorrow, graciously prepare my heart to receive Thy Word with meekness and the Spirit's work with joy. Let not the vanity of this present world turn me from Thee and the means of grace by which Thou grantest rich supplies from Thy heavenly treasures. I thank Thee for Thy love, my Father; let my whole life serve Thee. Amen.

Sunday

MORNING

✠

LORD Jesus, the Lover of my soul, take full possession of my heart today. Make me a dwelling place of Thy Holy Spirit. Preserve in me a clean heart which loves Thee and does Thy will at all times. Save me from the follies of sin and the despair of a guilty conscience. Keep me free from envy, discontent, bitterness, and strife. Banish all wicked desires from my heart, and grant that in word and deed I may honor Thee, who hast gone to the Cross to set me free from the power of Satan and sin. Strengthen and increase my faith, and lead me into the paths of righteousness, where I will serve Thee. Give me grace to grow in knowledge of Thee and of Thy Word that, living to Thee, I may die daily to sin and the world and serve Thee with all my heart. Abide with me, gracious Savior, that I may continue from day to day in Thy presence until life's journey is ended and I come into Thy presence to praise and glorify Thee, world without end. Amen.

Sunday

EVENING

✠

HEAVENLY Father, eternal God, by whose grace I live and by whose mercy I have been redeemed, look upon me with Thy favor, and remove from my heart and life all evil, worry, trouble, sorrow, and grief. Forgive me all my sins. In Thy love let me find peace; in Thy Word, hope; and in Thy promises, comfort and strength. Banish all sinful thoughts, and draw me with tender love closer to Thee. Let Thy Word, with which Thou hast fed our hungry souls today, at all times revive my faltering faith. Keep me throughout the night from every danger, and bless me with peaceful sleep that I may awake refreshed and strengthened to face the new day with all its problems and trials. Watch over the sick and the suffering, and let Thy divine presence fill them with hope and patience; through Jesus Christ, our Lord. Amen.

Monday

✠

ETERNAL God, who at no time dost forsake Thine own, take me by the hand, and lead me safely through this day. Have mercy upon me, and protect me from bitterness, confusion, suffering, disappointments, and the wickedness in this world of sin. Give me an unwavering faith which will hold fast to Jesus Christ as my Savior and Friend. Lift me to Thyself, and let Thy Holy Spirit breathe into my heart the joy of forgiveness and the peace that passeth all understanding. Grant me the grace to appreciate Thy Word and follow daily Thy precepts, believing Thy promises. Strengthen my faith. Guard me against the temptations that beset me, and make me hopeful, confident, cheerful, and courageous. I ask this in the name and for the sake of Jesus Christ, my Lord. Amen.

Monday

✠

LORD God, who art our Father in Christ Jesus, reconciled to me through His most precious blood, I come in this evening hour imploring Thy mercy and seeking Thy divine forgiveness. I can find no peace of heart and mind but in Thee, who hast sent Thy Son to the Cross with the burden of my guilt that I might be forgiven. Blot out each and every sin which I have committed today in thought, word, and deed. Thou knowest, O Lord, that they are many, and I know that they are grievous in Thy sight. But hide not Thy face from me, but be merciful, and receive me as Thine own, and embrace me with Thy love. Draw me closer to Thyself that I may find all my joy in Thee. In the shadow of Thy wings let me find protection for the night; through Jesus Christ, my Lord. Amen.

Tuesday

✠

O LORD, by whose grace I live and move and have my being, guide me through the coming hours of this day. Have mercy upon me, and help me as I face the bitterness, the confusion, and the ugliness of this world of sin. Preserve me from selfishness, greed, vanity, and pride. Teach me to be thoughtful toward those whom I meet today, and, above all, keep me in Thy divine love, which has reconciled me to Thee in Christ Jesus, my Lord. Lift me to Thy heart, and breathe upon me Thy Holy Spirit. Open my understanding that I may find joy and delight in Thy Word, which alone can sanctify my heart and mind. Keep me from temptation, and let sin have no power over me. Bless everything that I do, that by honest labor and work I may obtain my daily bread. Bless my food, my life, and my home, and keep me standing in Thy grace; through Christ Jesus, my All in all. Amen.

Tuesday

EVENING

✠

LORD Jesus, eternal Savior, hear Thou my prayers and supplications as I come in this evening hour seeking forgiveness of all my sins. They are many, and they have offended Thee. Fill my soul with peace. Take every complaint and rebellion out of my heart. Let Thy divine forgiveness make me forgiving. Reconcile those who are estranged from one another and from Thee. I thank Thee, gracious Savior, that Thou hast redeemed me and by Thy wonderful grace made me wise unto salvation. Keep me steadfast in this faith to the end of my days. I thank Thee for my daily bread and for each and every blessing which has come into our home. Watch over us this coming night, and let us awaken refreshed in body, confident of Thy mercy and goodness. This I ask of Thee as my Lord and Savior, as my Friend in every need and Helper in every trouble. Amen.

Wednesday

MORNING

✠

I BOW my head and heart, heavenly Father, to receive Thy benediction ere I go out into the world of toil and labor, sin and temptation. I need Thee as I seek my daily bread. Keep me content and confident. Let nothing disturb the peace of my heart and mind. Help me to resist and overcome the evil influences of the world. Let Thy Word direct my every thought and act. Shine Thou into my heart with Thy love, and bless me with Thy divine forgiveness. Bless the labors of my hands, and grant that I may glorify Thy name by walking in Thy ways and doing Thy will. Bless me as I enter and leave our home. Preserve me from every danger of body and soul. Keep me steadfast in the faith; then Thine shall be the praise and glory now and forever; through Christ Jesus, our Lord. Amen.

Wednesday

✠

I BOW my head to receive Thy benediction, eternal Caretaker of my body and soul, as I come to Thee at the close of this day. Shut out all sins that would cling to me, and wash me in Christ's precious blood from all my iniquities. Remove the worries and the cares of the day, and fill my soul with contentment and peace. Enter Thou into my heart, and take full possession that, standing in Thy grace, I may be faithful, trusting, and forgiving. Watch over me and over all Thine own during this coming night, and preserve our homes from danger and destruction. Bless all children and little babes, and let Thy divine presence give strength to the sick and consolation to the suffering. I ask this of Thee as my heavenly Father in the name of Jesus Christ, my Savior and Redeemer. Amen.

Thursday

✠

HEAVENLY Father, I come in Jesus' name asking Thee to take me by the hand and safely lead me through this day. Be Thou my Strength in this crooked and perverse world, my Stay in the hour of temptation, and my Refuge in every trouble. Keep me from sinning, and preserve me in faith. Fill my heart with the joy of forgiveness. Let me walk with Thee every hour of the day, hallowing Thy name by every word I utter and every act I do. Uphold me with Thine everlasting arms of mercy and goodness, and let me not be discouraged and disheartened by the trials and vexations of the day. Teach me to believe that Thou turnest everything to the good of those that love Thee. Keep before my eyes the suffering Savior. Let His undying love fill me with a greater love for Thee, and make me eager to confess Him as my Lord, who alone can bring peace to the soul and the hope of heaven to the heart. In His name and for His sake I ask this of Thee. Amen.

Thursday

EVENING

✠

In this evening hour I come to Thee, merciful Father, thanking Thee for the goodness and help which Thou hast shown me throughout the day. I am unworthy of all these Thy mercies, for I have sinned against Thee. Forgive me for Jesus' sake. Thou hast blessed the labors of my hands and brought me safely home for the night. Amid the vanities of life and the allurements of this world keep me standing in Thy grace. Make me humble, faithful, thankful. Let nothing be dearer to me than Thy Word, which makes me wise unto salvation. Keep me this night from every danger. Bless me with a quiet, restful sleep. Wherever anxious hearts are lifted up in prayer to Thee, incline Thine ear to them and grant them those things that they seek of Thee according to Thy gracious will. In life and death be Thou our God; for Jesus' sake. Amen.

Friday

✠

HEAVENLY Father, in the name of Jesus, our Savior, I approach Thee in this morning hour, beseeching Thee to let Thy grace and mercy go with me throughout the day. Let Thy presence give me the blessed assurance of Thy divine protection amid dangers, guidance amid uncertainty, and strength against temptations. Bless the labors of my hands. Bless our home with Thy continued presence. Bless our nation, and let righteousness and peace prevail. Bless Thy Church, and keep it in Thy Word and truth. Bless the schools, and grant that the boys and girls may grow in grace and knowledge of Thee and of Thy will. Remember not the sins of my youth nor my many trespasses. Bring me safely home tonight, and keep me steadfast in faith; through Jesus Christ, our Redeemer. Amen.

Friday

EVENING

✠

ETERNAL Savior, who hast given Thy life on the Cross to redeem us from sin and the fear of death, I seek Thy divine forgiveness and the peace that passeth all understanding. As the night closes in upon me, bless me with Thy gracious benediction. Blot out all my sins through Thy precious blood. Create in me a clean heart, filled with Thy Holy Spirit. Endow me with a deeper love for Thee and Thy Gospel. Let not the cares of the day rob me of restful sleep, nor let doubts and unbelief take from me the saving faith in Thee, who hast died that I might be Thine own eternally. I entrust myself to Thy safekeeping for the night, confident that Thou art my everliving and glorious Savior and King. Amen.

Saturday

✠

WITH grateful heart I come to Thee, O Lord, eternal God, because Thou hast so graciously preserved me throughout this night. In Thy tender love watch over me also this day. Guard me from sin, and keep me unshaken in the hour of temptation. Let not the vexing irritations of the day rob me of that hopeful spirit and that joy of heart which comes to me through Thy Word. Let Thy divine love enable me to glorify Thy name through every word and every act, and bring us all safely home in the evening hour. Watch over all those who trust in Thee, and forgive us as we come seeking Thy peace in Christ Jesus, our Lord. Bless our home and each member of our household. Keep me steadfast in the faith; through Christ Jesus, our Lord. Amen.

Saturday

✠

With grateful heart I come in this evening hour, faithful Father, because Thou hast so graciously preserved me throughout the day from many dangers of body and soul. Tenderly Thou didst guide me with Thine eye and hast kept me in the faith. Thou hast not left me to struggle alone with the cares and worries of life. Thou hast opened Thine hand and given me daily bread, which I acknowledge with thanksgiving to Thee, whose mercies are new every day. And yet I have been filled with anxious thoughts. Forgive me, gracious Lord. Blot out all my sins, and remember them no more. Grant me this night a peaceful rest, and let Thy divine love protect me. Watch over all Thy people, and be with the sick and the suffering in the still night watches. In Jesus' name I ask this of Thee, eternal Caretaker of our lives. Amen.

Sunday

✠

DEAR Lord, divine Jesus, in this hour, when Thy disciples throughout all the world are preparing to assemble to hear Thy holy Word and to worship Thee, my thoughts rise to Thee as the glorious Redeemer, through whose sacrifice I have been freed from the burden of sin and clothed in the garments of Thy perfect righteousness. Grant me the grace to sense that I owe my very life to Thee as I join my fellow Christians in hymns and prayers and in meditation of the glorious Gospel message. Keep from my mind distracting and unworthy thoughts. Let Thy divine truth be to me more precious than gold, yea, than much fine gold, and sweeter than honey and the honeycomb. Guide me through Thy Holy Spirit to be a doer and not only a hearer of Thy precious Gospel. Bless on this day my fellow believers and me for the sake of Thy great love. Amen.

Sunday

✠

As I come to the close of this Lord's day, I acknowledge, eternal God, Thy loving-kindness and grace, for Thou hast fed my soul with the heavenly Manna, the Gospel of reconciliation, and through Thy Word hast spoken peace to me in Thy love. Joy fills my heart as Thou graciously forgivest sin through Jesus Christ and strengthenest my faith through the indwelling of Thy Holy Spirit. Preserve me in the midst of a tempting world and a pleasure-minded people. Take me by the hand, and lead me safely through this coming week, providing me with the necessary food for each day and nourishing my soul with Thine everlasting Gospel; through Jesus Christ, my Savior and Lord. Amen.

Monday

✠

O THOU great God, my Creator and Preserver, I thank Thee from the depth of my heart for the gracious protection which Thou hast granted me in the past night, keeping all harm and danger from me and all those whom I love. As I prepare for the tasks of the day, I ask for Thy divine blessing and benediction. Let all my efforts prosper according to Thy holy and gracious will. Grant me help and strength for the work which has to be done; through Thy Holy Spirit help me to avoid whatever runs counter to Thy holy commandments; in the midst of all temptations keep alive in me the flame of faith in my blessed Redeemer. Enable me to render helpful service to my fellow men that Thou and Thy Word be praised and glorified. This I ask in the name of my Redeemer, Jesus Christ. Amen.

Monday

✠

Gracious God, Father, Son, and Holy Spirit, as this day draws to its close, I appear before Thee with thanksgiving, mindful of the many blessings which I have received from Thy bountiful hand. Thou hast been my Refuge and Fortress. No evil has befallen me; no plague has come nigh unto my dwelling. In humility I pray Thee, forgive me my many transgressions, my sinful desires and longings, my lack of zeal and devotion for Thy cause. Cover whatever I have done amiss with the garments of the righteousness prepared by my Lord and Savior Jesus Christ. Grant that I may ever seek safety in His sacred wounds. This night send Thy holy angels for my protection. I implore Thee to encompass with Thy mercy all my fellow men and to help them in their every need. Give them the best of all gifts, Thy Holy Spirit, that they may be led to life everlasting. Hear me for the sake of the Redeemer. Amen.

Tuesday

MORNING

✠

HEAVENLY Father, Thy love and mercy have safely taken me through another night, so that I am prepared for the duties of this new day. With a heart full of gratitude I acknowledge Thy protection. Thou didst not withhold from me Thy watchful care, unworthy though I be, but hast sought my well-being throughout the night. Withdraw not from me this day the presence of the Holy Spirit. Increase my faith in the Redeemer and my love toward Thee and my fellow men. If it please Thee, let my efforts be successful, and bless Thou the work of my hands. Help those who are in distress, dry the tears of those who weep, strengthen those who are feeble. Be a Father to all orphaned children. Build Thou Thy kingdom in this country and elsewhere to the glory of Thy name and the salvation of many immortal souls. Hear this my prayer for Jesus' sake. Amen.

Tuesday

✠

LORD God, merciful and gracious, as the hours of the night have come upon us, I thank Thee for the many blessings which Thou hast granted me this day. Thou hast not dealt with me according to my sins nor chastened me with Thy much-deserved corrections. As a father pitieth his children, so hast Thou in Thy compassion overlooked my many failings and shortcomings. Forgive me my trespasses. In the darkness which now encompasses us, be Thou with me and all those who are near and dear to me. Protect us from every approaching danger. Grant us the needed rest that will refresh and strengthen our bodies and minds. Let Thy holy angels protect Thy children wherever they may live. Where there is suffering, relieve it according to Thy will. Remove the spiritual blindness which keeps many away from the Savior, Thy dear Son, our Lord Jesus Christ, to whom with Thee and the Holy Spirit be glory and dominion forever and ever. Amen.

Wednesday

✠

DEAR Father in heaven, again Thou hast shown forth Thy loving-kindness by permitting me to rest in peace and to greet, strengthened and refreshed, the light of another day. Grant that I may never forget Thee as the Giver of all good and perfect gifts. Let me begin the day with the resolve to serve Thee in all sincerity of heart and loyal devotion. May Thy Holy Spirit constantly fill me with love for Thy precious Word. Let Him impart to my heart and mind thoughts, words, and deeds which are acceptable in Thy sight. As temptations come, help me to cling without wavering to my blessed Savior, who overcame the forces of hell on Calvary that I might live. Today give meat and drink to all mankind; open Thy hand and satisfy the desire of every living thing. Protect and prosper Thy holy Christian Church, with all its pastors, teachers, and missionaries, for the salvation of many immortal souls. I ask this in the name and for the sake of our dear Redeemer Jesus Christ. Amen.

Wednesday

EVENING

✠

GOD of might and mercy, with all Thy children I come before Thee in this evening hour, exalting Thee as my Father and Preserver, my Rock, my Fortress, and my Deliverer. Consider not my many sins and shortcomings, but graciously forgive them for the sake of my beloved Redeemer Jesus Christ. Let Thy Holy Spirit dwell in my heart that I may withstand and overcome all temptations of unbelief and worldliness. Let Him put pure and wholesome thoughts and desires into my heart. In the manifold dangers which beset us grant Thy strong protection to all who trust in Thee. Hear the cries of Thy children wherever they may be. Relieve the distress of those who are ill and hungry; check the ravages of wars, and let peace prevail on earth, that Thy holy Gospel may be preached in every nation and many souls be saved. This I ask in the name of Thy Son Jesus Christ, our Lord. Amen.

Thursday

✠

I WILL praise Thee, Lord, with my whole
heart; I will show forth all Thy marvelous
works. Thou providest health and strength,
courage and confidence, as the tasks of another
day come before me. Graciously protect me
from accidents and every form of sin and evil,
and bless the work of my hands. Grant me
help from above that I may prove to be a salt
and a light to my fellow men and fearlessly
confess my faith in Jesus Christ, my Redeemer.
In this world of wickedness and strife let the
Gospel of the peace which passeth all understanding be preached with power, that many
may find their Savior and be rescued from a life
of sin and an eternity of woe. Into Thy hands
I commend myself and all mankind, Thou
great Triune God, Father, Son, and Holy Spirit,
blessed forever. Amen.

Thursday

EVENING

✠

O GREAT God, who art merciful and gracious, long-suffering and abundant in goodness and truth, keeping mercy for thousands, forgiving iniquity and transgression and sin, again I have experienced in many ways Thy never-failing fatherly care and safely reached the end of another day. Grant that Thy love may lead my feet into the paths of Thy righteousness, where I will gratefully dedicate myself and my services to Thee. Give me the strength to resist more earnestly the allurements of sin. Forgive whatever I have done amiss, and protect me this night from every danger which might cause me harm and suffering. Let Thy mercy encompass all mankind in its manifold needs. Bring to naught the plans of evil men and of Satan. Keep all Thy children in the faith which joyfully relies on the merits of Jesus Christ, our Savior, and lead them, with many more to be won for Christ, to everlasting life; for the sake of our blessed Redeemer. Amen.

Friday

✠

HEAVENLY Father, with praise and joy I look up to Thee as the Helper and Deliverer who hast heard my prayers and in the night permitted no evil nor harm to touch me. Secure in Thy protection, I shall proceed to my daily tasks. Remove from my heart all pride and self-righteousness which might deny my sinful weakness and despise the merits of my divine Savior. Let the truths of Thy holy Word be precious in my sight, and help me to grow in understanding and knowledge of the Scriptures as I apply their precepts to my own life. Send Thy messengers with the Gospel of the redemption in Christ Jesus to many who are famished in the wilderness of this world, and lead them to the acceptance of the Bread of Life. Show them that now is the accepted time and the day of salvation. Hear this and all other requests of Thy children for the sake of Jesus, the Redeemer. Amen.

Friday

✠

THOU great and mighty God, Father, Son, and Holy Spirit, as the light of the day fades away and darkness covers the earth, I know that Thou who keepest Israel wilt neither slumber nor sleep. With thanksgiving I exalt Thee as the Source of the many blessings that have come upon me today. Teach me to see ever more clearly that life and happiness, health and daily bread, and peace of heart, forgiveness of sins, and the home in heaven are gifts of Thy divine grace. Continue Thy merices toward me, to all my friends and relatives, my fellow believers and all mankind. If I have enemies, bless them, and let them undergo a change of heart. Pardon all my transgressions and shortcomings for the sake of Jesus, my Redeemer. Strengthen Thy Church, and let its membership constantly grow and praise Thee, the only true God, here in time and hereafter in eternity. In Jesus' name. Amen.

Saturday

✠

Father of all mercies, who hast created, redeemed, and sanctified me, I extol Thy holy name as I enter upon this last day of the week. Thou hast graciously preserved me during the night. Be Thou likewise my Helper and Defender as the hours of the day advance. Give me strength and understanding for the tasks awaiting me and loyal devotion to the duties of my calling. Mercifully prosper the work of my hands. Keep me unselfish and loving in conduct. Help me to do to others what I should like to see them do to me. Let me remember that on earth I am a stranger and pilgrim, and teach me therefore to abstain from selfish lusts which war against the soul. Take all Thy children into Thy gracious hands, and teach them to walk as it becometh the profession of their faith. Let our fellow men know by our word and action that we belong to Jesus. This I ask in the name of my Lord Jesus Christ. Amen.

Saturday

✠

GREAT God of heaven, Thy fatherly protection has safely brought me to the end of another week. May I come, I pray Thee, to the close of the day with a repentant heart, mindful of my many failings and sins. Again I seek refuge in the Rock of Ages, cleft for me. Grant that through Thy Holy Spirit there may arise in me more powerfully than ever the resolve to deny myself, to take my cross, and to follow Jesus, my heavenly Lord and Master. Let Thy divine goodness accompany me on my pilgrimage as the weeks hasten on. Reveal Thyself as the Father of all the children of men, giving them bread and raiment, and opening Thy heart to forgive sin for the sake of thy beloved Son. As Thy Gospel is proclaimed throughout the world, make it effective in leading many souls to Christ as their only Redeemer, to whom with Thee and the Holy Spirit be honor and glory throughout eternity. Amen.

A General Morning Prayer

✠

In the name of the Father and of the Son
and of the Holy Ghost. Amen.

I THANK Thee, my heavenly Father, through Jesus Christ, Thy dear Son, that Thou hast kept me this night from all harm and danger; and I pray Thee that Thou wouldst keep me this day also from sin and every evil, that all my doings and life may please Thee. For into Thy hands I commend myself, my body and soul, and all things. Let Thy holy angel be with me, that the wicked Foe may have no power over me. Amen.

Luther's Small Catechism

A General Evening Prayer

✠

*In the name of the Father and of the Son
and of the Holy Ghost. Amen.*

I THANK Thee, my heavenly Father, through Jesus Christ, Thy dear Son, that Thou hast graciously kept me this day; and I pray Thee that Thou wouldst forgive me all my sins where I have done wrong, and graciously keep me this night. For into Thy hands I commend myself, my body and soul, and all things. Let Thy holy angel be with me, that the wicked Foe may have no power over me. Amen.

Luther's Small Catechism

Prayers

FOR CERTAIN TIMES AND SEASONS

Advent

✠

LORD Jesus, my Redeemer and King, as we celebrate the glorious advent of Thy coming into the world, I, Thy humble servant, open wide my heart to Thee. Cleanse and purify it from all sin and evil desire. So rule my life that I may yield the members of my body instruments of righteousness to Thee, my Lord. Give to the pastor of our congregation the necessary faithfulness, and grant success to all his endeavors. Fill the hearts of all the members with brotherly love toward one another and fervent zeal for the spreading of Thy Kingdom of Grace. Guard and protect Thy disciples against all error and falsehood, and heal all divisions and put to naught all heresies. Let Thy Church ever be a shining light to all the world. Deliver all whom Satan still holds in the bondage of unbelief and sin. And when Thou wilt appear in power and majesty at the end of time, grant that Thy glorious advent be to me a day of rejoicing and I lift up my head with gladness because my redemption draweth nigh. Amen.

Christmas Eve

✠

On the eve of Thy Nativity, adorable Savior, I come to Thee with the earnest prayer so to rule my entire heart and soul that I may celebrate Christmas in a manner pleasing to Thee and profitable to my own Christian life. Fill my heart with the genuine spirit of Christmas, which rejoices in the redemption from sin, the pardon of all iniquities, and the life eternal offered to all men at Thy manger. Let the significance of Christmas never be dwarfed by the manifold activities of the festive season, nor the worries and perplexing cares rob me of my Christmas joy. Thou, my Light and my Salvation, art come to me in yonder manger; whom, then, shall I fear? Lord Jesus, my Savior and my God, Thou hast given Thyself for me to cleanse me from all iniquity; grant that, standing at Thy lowly bed, I may ever look forward to Thy glorious appearing on that day when Thou wilt take me and all believers to the everlasting Christmas joy in our Father's home. Amen.

Christmas Day

✠

Jesus, my Savior, as I stand in spirit at Thy lowly manger, I bow my knees in reverent worship of that mystery without controversy great, revealed in Thy birth in Bethlehem's stable. Here lies God manifest in the flesh. O Jesus, teach me humbly to believe what reason cannot comprehend and with childlike faith to accept this mystery which no created mind can fully understand.

At Thy humble resting place, my Redeemer, I joyfully praise Thy love and grace. Thou hast left Thy Father's throne — for me. Thou hast taken the sins of the world upon Thyself — for me. Thou art willing to fulfill all righteousness — for me. Savior, I thank Thee for Thy unspeakable love, and I pray Thee, let me ever be faithful to Thee. As Thy love has drawn Thee from heaven to earth, so let Thy love draw me from earth to heaven to be Thine in time and eternity. Amen.

New Year's Eve

✠

LORD, make me to know mine end and the measure of my days that I may know how frail I am. Another year of my pilgrimage has passed. I am a year nearer to my death, nearer to Judgment, nearer to eternity to come. Whither shall I flee as the sins of the past year and the transgressions of the years rise to condemn me? Lord, to Thee I flee for refuge in these last hours of the waning year. For the sake of Thine own Son, whom Thou hast sent to be the Savior of all men, be gracious to me, and pardon mine iniquity. Trusting in the merits of my Savior, I come boldly to Thy throne of grace, in full confidence that there I shall obtain mercy and find grace to help in time of need. Oh, satisfy me early with Thy mercy that I may rejoice and be glad all my days. May the remaining years of my life be spent in Thy service that, when my last hour shall come, I may depart in peace to enter into Thy joy forevermore. Amen.

New Year's Day

✠

IT is of Thy mercies, O Lord, that I am not consumed, because Thy compassions fail not. They are new every morning; great is Thy faithfulness. Abide with me, O God, throughout the coming year. Be my Guide in all my perplexities, my Strength in weakness, my ever-ready Help in all my troubles. Forgive me all my sins. Look down from heaven, I beseech Thee, God of Hosts; behold and visit with Thy grace Thy holy Christian Church, which Thou hast chosen for Thine own. Preserve to it Thy Word and Sacraments, that Thy vine may send out its boughs from sea to sea and its branches to the uttermost parts of the earth. Look graciously upon our native land and all the nations of the world, and bless them with peace. Grant to all that are in authority wisdom and courage so to rule that we may lead a quiet and peaceful life in all godliness and honesty. To Thine almighty and gracious providence I commit our nation, our Church, our families, myself. Abide with me with Thy grace and mercy, and preserve my whole spirit and soul and body blameless to the coming of my Lord Jesus Christ. Amen.

Epiphany

✠

ARISE, my soul, and shine, for thy Light, the Savior Jesus Christ, is come to thee, and the glory of the Lord is risen upon thee. O loving Savior, may my soul never forget Thy blessings so abundantly shed upon me. Thou hast revealed Thyself to me also and given me the knowledge of salvation by the remission of my sins through Thy blood shed on Calvary. Alas, how neglectful have I been in the performance of my duty and my privilege of bringing the glad tidings of salvation to my fellow sinners! Forgive my sluggishness and indifference. Open Thou my lips and my hands, and give me a prayerful heart that I may become a salt and a light to my fellow men. Kindle in me and in all Thy children a fervent love for the souls of perishing sinners, and grant Thy blessing to all we say and do and offer, that Thy Kingdom of Grace may come to every nation and kindred and people, to the glory of Thy name and the salvation of souls purchased by Thy blood. Hear us for Thine own sake, Thou glorified Savior. Amen.

Lent

✠

LORD Jesus, precious Savior, who didst go all the way to the Cross to redeem me, a lost and condemned creature, graciously look upon me in this Lenten season, and let me find cleansing and healing in Thy precious blood. My transgressions have caused Thee the agony of the Garden. My sins have nailed Thee to the accursed tree. Thou wast forsaken that I be not forsaken throughout all eternity. Make me see the awfulness of my sin and then Thy wondrous love that would not let me die.

Grant that I may ponder day after day upon Thy Passion. Let nothing distracting take my thoughts from Thee. Draw me closer to Thee that I might find in Thee forgiveness and peace.

Bless this Lenten season in our many Christian congregations. Grant to the pastors grace to proclaim Thy glorious Passion with consecrated hearts, that all who hear this message of reconciliation may love Thee more and more. Abide with our household, and let sin have no dominion over us. Beholding Thee dying for our transgressions, may we live to Thee today and tomorrow and forever. Amen.

Ash Wednesday

✠

GRACIOUS Savior, prostrate I fall at Thy feet this day as Thy Christian Church and all Thy believers enter once more the Lenten season to ponder upon Thy Passion, by which we have been eternally redeemed.

In spirit I appear before Thee in sackcloth and ashes; in true repentance let me receive Thy full pardon. Let not the pleasures of life, the worries of the day, the activities of our daily routine, crowd Thee out of my heart and out of my thoughts. Draw me to Thy wounded side, and cleanse me with Thy most precious blood. Bring healing to my soul and peace to my mind. By Thy grace let me crucify my sinful affections, lusts, and desires. Make me more than conqueror over every temptation which besets me.

I confess to Thee all my sins. Let none of them cling to me. Create in me a clean heart. Teach me to love Thee more and more. Give me grace to confess Thee as my Savior, who hast redeemed me on Calvary, lifting me out of the darkness of sin to be Thine own. Gracious Savior, let Thy constraining love keep me and all Thy children steadfast to the end. Amen.

Palm Sunday

✠

LORD Jesus, King of my heart, today again I praise Thee with my hosannas and welcome Thee as the Lover of my soul. Come to my heart and take full possession. As thousands and ten thousands today vow faithfulness to Thee until death, acknowledging that they have no other Savior, grant that I, too, join this great host of faithful people to renew the covenant that once I made and dedicate myself anew to Thee as my Lord and King.

I confess, gracious Savior, that I have not been as true to Thee as Thou hast been to me. Other interests have placed themselves above Thee in my thoughts. Forgive me, O Lord. Accept my homage. Give me grace and strength to walk closer to Thee and serve Thee more faithfully by consecrating my life, my heart, my all, to Thee, who hast loved me unto death. Gracious Savior, draw me closer and closer to Thee. Preserve me in the faith until the end of days that I may behold Thee in glory forevermore. Hear my cry, King of my heart and Savior of my soul. Amen.

Monday

✠

PRECIOUS Savior, Lamb of God for sinners slain, graciously forgive me all my sins, and embrace me with Thy tender love. My love has not always been warm and ardent and true. This I confess, O Lord. The love of life, the allurements of the present world, the glamour of success, the favor of friends, have enticed me away from Thee. These things would take possession of my heart. O Lord, let me not sell my soul for the passing treasures of this present world. If I have kissed Thee with the kiss of betrayal, kiss Thou me with the kiss of forgiveness, and embrace me again as Thine own. Have mercy upon me!

Protect me from the cunning of Satan, the allurements of the world, and the wickedness of my own heart. Thou art my surest Friend; hold me lest I stumble and fall. Guard my heart that the love of gold, the smiles of popularity, the eagerness to succeed, may not rob me of my salvation, which Thou hast so dearly bought with

Thine own blood. Above all, gracious Savior, let me not despair of Thy mercy, but believe at all times that Thy love is as boundless as the heavens and deeper than the esa. O Friend of sinners, let me not fall away from Thee. Keep me standing in Thy grace until I shall stand in Thy presence forevermore, to love Thee with a perfect love throughout all eternity. Amen.

Tuesday

✠

LORD Jesus, compassionate Savior, plead for me in the hour of trial. Thou knowest my weaknesses and shortcomings, I cannot hide my sins from Thee. Pray for me, gracious Redeemer, lest I deny Thee.

O Lord, Thou knowest that I have promised to be faithful to Thee, and nevertheless I have again and again sinned and offended Thee with my many transgressions. I am ashamed of myself. Yet I come to Thee. I have denied Thee, if not by word, then by my actions and conduct. O Lord, look upon me in mercy, and forgive me all my sins.

I have not always confessed Thee to the world nor spoken of the hope within me. Gracious

Savior, forgive me in Thy great love. Do not let me go on in my sin. Look into my heart, and make me ashamed of myself and truly penitent.

O Lord, Thou knowest that I love Thee. Thine I am. Help me to be more faithful, more devout, more zealous. In this Holy Week lead me to a deeper appreciation of the great sacrifice whereby Thou hast redeemed me.

And, Lord, in Thy mercy look up all erring, sinning, straying children of Thine, and bring them back and restore them to grace. Draw us all to Thee with Thy constraining love, and keep us steadfast, unfaltering, and true. Hear my petitions and prayers, O Lover of my soul. Amen.

Wednesday

✠

LORD Jesus, gracious Savior, I come to Thee in this sacred week to ponder upon Thy great, wondrous love, which led Thee to the Cross that my sin might be blotted out and I be reconciled to my heavenly Father. O Christ, give me strength and grace to crucify my sinful desires and dedicate myself anew to Thee, who hast loved me with an everlasting love and brought to me eternal salvation.

I confess to Thee my sins. They are many, and Thou knowest them all. For each and every one of them Thou hast suffered the agony of the Cross and shed Thy precious blood that I may be cleansed and made acceptable in Thy sight. Let me not go through this day unmindful of Thy great love. Let none of the sins of yesterday cling to me. Humbly I come, seeking Thy mercy. Daily let me go forth in the world in which I live to serve Thee and confess Thee as my Lord and Savior.

Grant that Thy suffering and death, proclaimed for the salvation of mankind, may by the power of the Holy Spirit awaken in many a deeper love to Thee. O Lord, have mercy upon me and all sinful mankind, and create in me and all that seek Thee a clean heart, holy desires, and an undying love. Hear my prayer, gracious Redeemer. Amen.

Maundy Thursday

✠

ETERNAL Savior, how can my heart show its appreciation of Thy love? How can I serve Thee best, who hast loved me and given Thy life for me? Thou hast sealed unto me the forgiveness of all my sins and offered me reconciliation and peace in the blesesd Sacrament which Thou didst institute on this day. Thou hast promised to give me with the bread and the cup Thy body and blood for the remission of all my sins. Oh, what amazing love! What riches of divine wisdom! In awe and wonderment I ponder upon this gracious gift. May I ever appreciate this blessed Sacrament that Thou hast bidden me to use oft in remembrance of Thee. May I come worthily each time when I approach Thine altar.

O Savior, cast me not away from Thy presence. Let not my sins remain with me because of impenitence of heart or because I doubt Thy Word and promises. Let me become one with Thee and all Thy saints as I receive with them this blessed Sacrament. Make me Thine, and give me strength to amend my sinful life and walk closer to Thee.

Preserve in Thy Christian Church this blessed Sacrament given on this sacred day. Let thousands and ten thousands find through it the assurance of forgiveness, peace, and salvation. And grant to me and all those that are Thine to be faithful to Thy Word and Sacraments, that Thy name be glorified, Thy will be done, and we at last live with Thee in Thine eternal kingdom, Thine forevermore. Amen.

Good Friday

✠

O CHRIST, Thou Lamb of God, slain for the sin of the whole world, with penitent heart I come to Thy Cross, pleading for mercy and forgiveness. My sins — and they are many — have added to the burden of Thy suffering and have nailed Thee to the accursed tree. For me Thou hast tasted the agony of the utter darkness that I might not perish, but have everlasting life. Have mercy upon me.

O Christ, Thou Lamb of God, embrace me with Thy love, and forgive me all my sins. Thy death brings healing to my soul, peace to my mind, cleansing to my heart. If Thou wouldst mark iniquity, I could not come; for my hands are unclean, my lips are sullied, and my heart is blackened by sin. But beholding Thee bleeding, despised, forsaken, dying, pierced, I come to be cleansed and forgiven.

O Christ, Thou Lamb of God, grant that I may hate sin and wickedness more and more as I behold Thee in Thy great agony. My grateful heart today finds hope in Thy words, comfort in Thy promises, salvation in Thy finished work on the Cross, by which Thou hast overcome sin, Satan, and death.

O Christ, Thou Lamb of God, grant that I may daily walk by faith, crucifying all sinful desires and giving myself and dedicating my all to Thee. Keep me faithful to the end of my days, until I stand before Thy throne to worship Thee, the Lamb once slain but now living and reigning forever, adored by the multitude of heaven. Hear my cry, Redeemer of my soul. Amen.

Saturday

✠

DIVINE and everliving Savior, Thou didst go into the grave to make death a sleep from which our mortal bodies shall arise on the Last Day. We shall live because Thou livest. Let me look forward with joy to the day of my departure, confidently believing that I shall rise from the dust of the earth with a body like unto Thy glorious body. Be with me when my last hour cometh.

Forgive me all my sins, fill my soul with peace. Make me unafraid of the Judgment to come, knowing that there is no condemnation for them that believe. O death, where is thy sting? I thank Thee, Lord, for Thine eternal victory over death and the grave.

Comfort the hearts of those who are sorrowing because the angel of death has crossed the threshold of their homes and taken a precious soul out of their midst. Hold out to them through Thy Word the glory of heaven, when by Thine infinite grace they shall see Thee and those who are Thine gathered around Thine eternal throne.

Give me daily the blessed assurance that heaven is my home. Make me watchful and wakeful. Keep me on the narrow way which leads me to eternal glory. Give me the grace to say with confident assurance: I believe in the resurrection of the body and the life everlasting. Abide with me day by day until I, now believing, shall see Thee face to face forevermore. Amen.

Early Easter Morning

✠

LORD Jesus, everliving Friend, bring to my remembrance as I awaken from my sleep this morning, how Thou didst on this first day rise from the dead. Fill my heart with the perfect joy and the abundant trust in the glory of Thy resurrection. May Thy Gospel this day speak sureness and peace to my soul. Let men everywhere be quickened to a newness of faith and life by the power of Thy resurrection. Give me the strength to overcome every force of darkness and walk with Thee in true righteousness. Amen.

Easter

✠

LORD Jesus, risen gloriously from the dead, I worship Thee as my living Savior, who hast redeemed me to be Thine own eternally; and I adore Thee as Conqueror of Satan, sin, and death. Accept me and my Easter hallelujah, which I bring to Thee with all believers of all ages and races and nations.

Joy fills my heart as I come into Thy presence; for Thy resurrection proclaims to me and all believers forgiveness of all our sins, which brings peace to our hearts and songs of praise to our lips. I know that we are now reconciled to God, our heavenly Father.

Joy fills my heart as I worship Thee, the eternal, living Lord; for death cannot hold us in terror, and even the grave cannot keep our dust and ashes. I need not weep despairing tears; for Thou wilt raise me and all believers to eternal life. Our loved ones fallen asleep in Thee are in Thy safekeeping, eternally delivered from this world of suffering and pain.

Joy fills my heart as I today join with all Thy people to praise Thee; for I know that the gates of hell shall not prevail against Thy Church, which by Thy power and strength goes on from victory to victory as we bear witness of Thee and confess Thy name to the ends of the earth.

Take full possession of my heart today. Cleanse me from all sin. Keep me in Thy grace. Let not the cares and worries of life rob me of the joy of Thy Gospel. Increase the number of Thy faithful people from day to day. Gather from all nations of the earth Thine own elect. Then Thine shall be the glory, Thine the honor, Thine the praise, throughout all eternity. Amen. Hallelujah! Amen.

Ascension

✠

LORD Jesus, who didst on the day of Thy ascension withdraw Thy visible self from the eyes of Thy disciples, yet hast promised to be with them always unto the end of the world, and now fillest and rulest all things, I adore Thy great majesty and entreat Thee to let Thy presence and love enrich my life from day to day. Through Thy Word and Spirit make Thy presence felt even unto the end of days. Let Thy Word and Sacrament be mighty means for the strengthening of my faith in Thy abiding presence. Let not doubt and questionings within my heart and life nor the woes and chaos in the world make me question Thy power to save and to rule; strengthen my conviction that Thou dost direct all things for good to Thy Church, of which Thou art the Head. Above all, fill my heart with longing for that heavenly home whither Thou hast gone to prepare a place for me, and give me a strong desire and watchful readiness for the day when I shall see Thee coming again to take me into Thy mansions above. In Thy name I ask it. Amen.

Pentecost

✠

HOLY Spirit, divine Comforter, sent into
the world to give knowledge of God and understanding of heavenly things, give me a clearer
and better understanding of the riches and the
power of God and of the way of life which is
found in Christ Jesus, our Lord. Take Thou full
possession of my mind, and use me for Thy
purposes and service. Help me to conquer every
doubt and all dismay, all hatred of the world
and wickedness of man.

O Holy Spirit, make all things new in my
life; make me truly reborn to God. Free me
from every taint of the sinful flesh, and give me
strength to conquer all temptations to sin and
all fears and doubts. Through the power of
Thine indwelling make me more perfect in following the ways of Jesus, Thou who hast made
us Christ's own through faith in His precious
blood.

Most precious Spirit, be Thou my everlasting
Guide as I travel to the city of God which is in
heaven. As Thou hast raised me from spiritual
death to life in Christ and hast made me new
to God, so assure to me also a rising from the

bodily death to an eternal life in the heavenly mansions. Spirit of God, live in me day after day, and with the Father and the Son make Thine abode in me forevermore. Amen.

Pentecost—For the Church

✠

HOLY Spirit, who on that first Pentecost didst establish by Thy outpouring upon the disciples at Jerusalem the Christian Church, I thank Thee that through Thy Word and Sacrament Thou hast continued Thy Church through the ages and preserved the fellowship of the faithful throughout the years. I pray Thee, grant me so firm a faith in the Redeemer, and so steadfast a fruitfulness in Thy service, that through me and our generation Thou mightest build Thy Church among the children of men. Protect us from all falsehood and error. Heal all controversies and dissensions, and hasten the day of a God-pleasing union of all Christian people. Grant all of us grace to be loyal to Thy Word, resisting all efforts to set aside Thy revealed Truth. Take all indifference out of our hearts, and make us zealous instruments of Thy Church, that many souls be added to Christ's kingdom through our testimony. May through Thy grace young and old by word and deed bear witness of the hope within them and of Thy glorious indwelling, in Jesus' name. Amen.

Trinity Sunday

✠

THOU great Triune God, Father, Son, and Holy Spirit, our Creator, Redeemer, and Sanctifier, with reverent awe and admiration I look up to Thee and join in the song of the angels: Holy, holy, holy, is the Lord of Hosts, the whole earth is full of His glory! I praise Thee as the Source of all our blessings. In Thee we live and move and have our being. Thou hast provided a sacrifice for all our sins and opened again for us the gates of Paradise, which were closed by our transgressions. Through Thee the flame of faith has been lit in my heart that I am again a child of Thy grace. With grateful heart I look up to Thee, saying: Abba, Father. In mercy Thou daily forgivest all of my sins and suppliest strength that I, though with halting steps, walk the way of Thy Commandments. Heavenly Lord, who art One in Three, grant that I may ever and always accept the mysteries of Thy

Being, as revealed in Thy holy Word. Increase the numbers of those who behold Thy majesty in faith and bow before Thee, of whom and through whom and to whom are all things. I ask it in the name of Jesus, my Savior. Amen.

Reformation Sunday

✠

HEAVENLY and divine Savior, Bishop and Ruler of the Church, I thank Thee this day for Thine unchanging grace by which Thou hast preserved to us Thy glorious Gospel of reconciliation and made us heirs of eternal glory. I thank Thee for Thy many mercies throughout the years by which Thou hast upheld Thy Church amid persecution and defeat. Thou hast given to the Church mighty leaders and defenders of the truth. I acknowledge Thy goodness and grace toward us. I thank Thee for the privilege of membership in Thy Church Universal into which I am born through Thy Holy Spirit. I rejoice in the fellowship with all who, following in the footsteps of the saints of old, are dedicated to the truth that we are saved by grace, through faith, in Thy redeeming sacrifice.

I entreat Thee, most merciful Bishop of souls,

continue the blessings coming forth from Thy unerring Word and the privilege of my fellowship with faithful people. Teach me to use the talents entrusted to me with fervent testimony, dauntless courage, and hallowed zeal. I give myself to the task of bringing the saving message of forgiveness to the world and thereby give evidence of my loyal devotion to Thee. Kindle in me a greater love that I may serve Thee as the heroes of faith of yesteryears. I ask this in the name of Jesus, the Author and Finisher of our faith. Amen.

Thanksgiving Day

✠

GREAT and merciful God and Father, of whom the whole family in heaven and earth is named, on this day of our national thanksgiving I appear before Thee with gratitude in my heart and praise upon my lips. I extol Thee who hast opened Thy hands to supply our needs and Thy heart to forgive us our many sins. Thou hast permitted our fields to be tilled, the seed to be sown, the grain to ripen, the harvest to be gathered, gardens and orchards to give their yield. Thou hast prospered industries and business. Thou hast blessed the labors of our hands.

I pray Thee of Thy boundless mercy and for the sake of the holy, innocent, bitter sufferings and death of Thy beloved Son, Jesus Christ, to be gracious and merciful to me, a poor sinful being. Amen.

Prayer for College Students

✠

HEAVENLY Father, who Thyself art Wisdom and givest light to the understanding of mankind, shine Thou into my heart with that knowledge which will give me a fuller appreciation of Thy Word, a saner outlook upon life, and a surer confidence in Thy over-all guidance through this day. Give me a greater measure of faith, and by that faith peace of mind, hope, and stability for tomorrow, and an escape from the uncertainties and doubts arising again and again in my youthful heart.

Pour out upon me Thy benedictions, and grace my day with Thy presence. Forgive me in Thy mercy wherever I have acted contrary to Thy will, and take me by the hand, and lead my footsteps into the paths of Thy righteousness.

Let me find joy in my studies, and help me to understand the subjects for which I am preparing myself today. Above all, let me grow in grace and be firmly established in Thy Word, which alone can make me wise unto salvation.

Mercifully protect me from unbelief and doubt, and give me the needed strength to resist the temptations which beset me on all sides. Grant that nothing separate me from my Savior, who has purchased me with His atoning sacrifice on Calvary. Give me the courage to acknowledge Him as the Redeemer of my soul and the Lord of my life at all times and in all places.

Then Thine shall be the honor and the glory and the praise arising from my grateful heart now and always. Amen.

For Our Colleges and Seminaries

✠

O THOU God of peace, who hast brought again from the dead our Lord Jesus, that great Shepherd of the sheep, we pray Thee in behalf of the institutions established in our midst for the training of pastors and shepherds of Thy flock which Thy Son has redeemed through the everlasting blood of the covenant. It is Thy will that the men serving as pastors and teachers in Thy Christian Church be faithful men, able to teach others, examples to the flock. To this end we commit to Thy gracious care all our colleges and seminaries. Give the instructors a double portion of Thy Holy Spirit. Pour out upon them a full measure of Christian humility, which in childlike submission to Thy eternal wisdom will bring into captivity every thought to the obedience of Christ and His Word. Let all instruction and training constantly be permeated by that fear of the Lord and obedience to Thy Word which is the beginning of all wisdom. Give to all the students willingness to receive Thy Word and with a prayerful mind and with all diligence to apply themselves to their studies and tasks. By Thy Holy Spirit furnish them thoroughly to all good works, that they may become consecrated leaders of Thy flock and ably assist Thy Son in leading many souls to glory. In Jesus' name. Amen.

For the Christian Day School

✠

LORD Jesus, Thou art the Savior of all mankind, young and old, who desirest that the lambs as well as the sheep of Thy flock be fed by Thy shepherds. To this end Thou hast charged Thy Church to disciple all nations, baptizing them in the name of the Father and of the Son and of the Holy Ghost, teaching them to observe all things whatsoever Thou hast commanded them. In keeping with this Thy will we have established a Christian day school in our midst where the children given into our care may be brought up in the nurture and admonition of the Lord. We implore Thy continued blessing upon our school, its teachers, and its pupils. Give us at all times God-fearing, faithful teachers who willingly and patiently will instruct the children entrusted to their care, teaching them the way of life and all useful learning and wisdom of this world. Let Thy holy Word fall like fruitful seed into the hearts and minds of the children, and bring them to the saving knowledge of Thee, the only true God, and of Jesus Christ, whom Thou hast sent. Give them the grace to set their hope and trust in Thee, that they may keep Thy Commandments and walk in Thy ways and remain faithful, loyal members of Thy Church on earth until Thou wilt call them to Thy everlasting kingdom of glory. Amen.

For My Sunday School

✠

JESUS, Thou art the Friend of children and dost not desire that one of these little ones should perish. Therefore Thou hast charged Thy Church to suffer the little children to come unto Thee. We therefore commit to Thee our Sunday school, the attending children, the teachers, and all others working therein. Thou alone canst create faith and hope and love in the hearts of these children. Thou alone canst preserve them in faith against all the evil influences from without. I pray Thee, give Thy divine blessing to the instruction offered in our Sunday school. May Thy Word become in all pupils a well of water springing up into everlasting life. Enable them to walk as Christians in this sinful world. Grant that the teachers at all times realize the importance of their task, teaching the way of life to the children whom Thou hast bought with Thy holy, precious blood. Give them the ability to teach the way of salvation that every child may clearly perceive and understand. May the lives of the teachers at all times be shining examples of Christian virtues. I ask Thee, hear my prayer for Thine own sake. Amen.

For the Church at Large

✠

LORD Jesus Christ, King and God, who in this world of unrest and strife hast founded Thy Holy Christian Church as a kingdom of peace and joy, I thank Thee who hast established this great world-wide communion of saints in which all believers are joined by the invisible but precious bond of faith in Thee as the only Redeemer. I thank Thee that Thou hast made me a citizen in this Thy holy kingdom and praise Thee who in Thy goodness hast bestowed upon me and all Thy children the richest and fairest of all gifts, Thy Holy Spirit. Keep alive in all the flame of faith. Fill us again and again with the spirit of love and peace toward one another. Make us in an increasing measure the salt of the earth and the light of the world, and fulfill Thy promise at this time that the gates of hell shall not prevail against Thy Church. Extend this kingdom of Thine that "the abundance of the sea shall be converted unto Thee, the forces of the Gentiles shall come unto Thee." Hear us for Thy truth's sake. Amen.

For Missions at Home

✠

GREAT God, Father, Son, and Holy Spirit, who dost not desire the death of the transgressor, but that sinners should turn from their evil way and live, I humbly ask Thee to remember in mercy and love the many unchurched people in this fair land of ours, especially those who have never learned the way of salvation. Lead them to the knowledge of the truth. Grant that the messengers of Thy Gospel may reach many and bring them the sweet tidings of Thy redeeming grace. Let those who read the Holy Scriptures find in them forgiveness and eternal life. All those who bring the message of reconciliation to these our fellow citizens who are still outside the gate, I commend to Thy heavenly protection and ask Thee to make their word powerful and effective. Gather the lost into the fold of the Good Shepherd of our souls. I ask this in the name of our blessed Redeemer, Jesus Christ. Amen.

For Missions Abroad

✠

O THOU mighty Lord, whose Son died on the Cross to redeem all the children of men, those who are near and those who are far off, I pray Thee to look with compassion upon the millions of my fellow men who are still sitting in the darkness and shadow of death, with immortal souls still lost, dead in trespasses and sin. Blinded, they cannot find Thee. Dead, they cannot rise to newness of life. Grant that the missionaries may reach them with the message of the Cross that they may believe and live. Wherever consecrated men and women are engaged in the blessed task of bringing the Gospel to the heathen, do Thou give success to their labors. Open the hearts of many to receive the saving Word of reconciliation. Establish Thy Church in the midst of the enemies, and let the fruits of true righteousness abound. Give Thy protection to all our missionaries abroad, and ward off all persecution. Keep them healthy and strong in body and mind. Give them the grace to be patient and faithful, and finally receive them and those whom they lead to Christ into the glory of heaven. I ask it in His name. Amen.

For the Ministers of the Word

✠

LORD Jesus, divine Savior and Helper, Thou hast established in Thy Church the office of the holy ministry that Thy Word may be preached and the Sacraments administered to the salvation of immortal souls. I pray Thee, grant to Thy ministers wisdom and strength and faithfulness in the performance of the many duties of their holy calling. Make them fearless witnesses of Thy truth, instant in season and out of season. Keep them from error and deceptions. Make their preaching effective, their admonition sympathetic, and instructions lucid. Grant that they be patient toward the weak, helpful toward the distressed, loving toward the erring. Give them strength to walk in the way of Thy Commandments and to be an example of Christian living to all men. May Thy Church through their work be established far and wide. Give to the members of our congregations grace to honor their pastors and gladly accept from them the divine Word and instruction. Keep them and us hearers faithful unto death, and give us in the end a crown of life. In Thy name I ask it. Amen.

For the Teachers of the Church

✠

LORD Jesus, ascended and everliving Lord, Thou hast given Thy Church many precious gifts, teachers who expound the Word and lead others to the knowledge of the truth. Thou hast given Thy Church men and women who give unselfishly of their leisure and time to the teaching of Thy saving Gospel. Bless them as they open to others the sacred Scriptures with the message of redemption through Thy blood. Let them seek nothing but Thine honor, glorifying Thee as the true God and the eternal Life. Give them the ability to instruct the simple, to strengthen the weak, and to refute the gainsayers. Preserve them from every error which runs counter to Thy holy revelation. May they lead many to righteousness by Thy grace and finally as faithful servants receive the crown of everlasting and heavenly glory. Hear us for the sake of Thy promises. Amen.

For the Congregation

✠

HEAVENLY Father, who hast heard our daily prayer "Thy kingdom come" and through the Holy Spirit hast made us Thy children, a chosen generation, a royal priesthood, a holy nation, I thank Thee that in our community Thou hast established a Christian congregation in which Thy Word is proclaimed in its completeness and fullness and Thy Sacraments are administered as Thou hast instituted them. Above all do I acknowledge Thy mercy in bringing me into fellowship with this congregation. Blessing upon blessing dost Thou shower upon us as we come before the throne. I pray Thee, continue to bless this church in Thy goodness and grace. Make effective the preaching of Thy Word, let our prayers come before Thee as incense, keep alive and active in us the spirit of brotherly love and helpfulness, stifle in us every improper ambition and sinful pride. Teach us to weep with those who suffer and to rejoice with those who are honored and happy. Add to our membership a large number of those who travel with us the road of life, and keep us in the narrow way which leads to life eternal. Hear us for the sake of Thy dear Son. Amen.

Before Confession and Absolution

✠

O LORD, merciful and mighty, I, an unworthy sinner, come to Thee in humble repentance and confess to Thee the many transgressions of Thy holy Law of which I am guilty. Forgive my iniquities and many shortcomings for the sake of the suffering and death of my Savior Jesus Christ. Let His obedience cover my disobedience, let His righteousness atone for my unrighteousness. Great God and Helper, Thou offerest me the forgiveness of my sins in the words of absolution. With all my heart I thank Thee for this Thy boundless mercy. Grant that I may accept this divine gift in sincere faith and look upon the word of pardon as a message coming from Thee. Let me treasure at all times this absolution, and let it bring forth works of obedience and love in my life day after day. Grant this for the sake of my divine Redeemer. Amen.

Before Holy Communion

✠

GRACIOUS Lord Jesus, in divine love Thou hast instituted in the Upper Room for me Thy Sacred Supper, in which Thou offerest me the very means by which Thou hast procured my salvation, Thy holy body and Thy precious blood. Thereby Thou assurest me of the reality of Thy death and the blessed fruits of the Cross, the redemption of the world and the forgiveness of all our sins. I thank Thee with joyful heart for this covenant of grace, pledging to me that sin and death have been overcome and that for all men, and for me, the gates of heaven have been opened wide, which no man can shut. As the hour approaches when I am to be a guest at Thy Table, give me through Thy Spirit's guidance a truly repentant heart. Make me mindful of my unworthiness and my many transgressions. Give me the grace to rely altogether on Thy merits and receive with gratitude Thy heavenly gifts. In all humility, O Lord, I dedicate my entire life anew to Thy service. Hear me for the sake of Thy bitter suffering and death. Amen.

Before Communion

✠

DEAREST Savior, who dost bend down in divine compassion and love to me as I prepare to receive, with the bread and the cup of the Sacrament, Thy most holy body and blood, grant me a faith which will not doubt the truth of Thy words: "This is My body given for you," "This is My blood shed for you." Shut out all worldly thoughts as I meditate upon Thy mercy, Thy suffering and dying in my stead.

> *Just as I am, without one plea*
> *But that Thy blood was shed for me*
> *And that Thou bidd'st me come to Thee,*
> *O Lamb of God, I come, I come.*

O Christ, Thou Lamb of God, be merciful to me, a sinner. Lord, I believe; help Thou mine unbelief. Amen.

After Holy Communion

✠

MERCIFUL Redeemer, Thou hast fulfilled Thy promise upon me: "Come unto Me, all ye that labor and are heavy laden, and I will give you rest." At Thy Table I have received nourishment for my soul and refreshment in my weariness. By giving me, with the bread and the cup, Thy body and Thy blood, Thou hast again said to me: "Fear not, for I have redeemed thee; I have called thee by thy name; thou art Mine." Thou hast blotted out all my iniquities and put on me the garments of Thy righteousness. Make me truly grateful and appreciative of Thy love. Through this Sacrament give me power to overcome unbelief and doubt, conquer temptations and evil desires, and produce in me works of righteousness and of humble service. Returning from Thy Table, may I with eager zeal dispense the Bread of Life to my fellow men that they may share with me the joy and happiness of Thy forgiving love. To Thee and the Father and the Holy Spirit be glory forever and ever. Amen.

On the Day of Confirmation
of a Child

✠

FAITHFUL and gracious Lord, Thou hast granted to us the joy of beholding our son (our daughter) confess his (her) faith in Thee, the only true God, Father, Son, and Holy Ghost. We beseech Thee to keep him (her) faithful to Thee all the days of his (her) life.

O Lord, we, too, dedicate our lives again to Thee and ask Thee to give us strength and grace to live closer to Thee, who hast so graciously been with us throughout these many years. We confess that we have not always served Thee as we ought; forgive us and grant that we may walk daily in Thy presence as an example of Christian devotion and consecrated living to our son (daughter). Preserve and keep us in Thy grace, and make our home Thy dwelling place, where Thy Word governs our every thought, word, and deed.

O Lord, let this day be a day of rejoicing to all who confess Thee. We ask this in Jesus' name. Amen.

In Memory of Confirmation

✠

GOD Father, Son, and Holy Spirit, Thy grace in Holy Baptism delivered me from the power of darkness and translated me into the kingdom of Thy dear Son. Thy grace, too, led me into the Holy Scriptures, which are able to make me wise unto salvation through faith which is in Christ Jesus. In that solemn hour when I renewed my baptismal covenant and again pledged faithfulness to the Savior and His Gospel, it was Thy Holy Spirit that supported me and helped me make a good confession. Grant, I pray Thee, that I may ever remember the promises I made on the day of my confirmation. Let the truths of the Holy Scriptures with the message of forgiveness and peace be my guide throughout all the days of my life. Protect me against the poison of impurity, wickedness, and unbelief. Take not Thy Holy Spirit from me. Keep me faithful unto death, that I may receive the crown of life eternal. Do this for Jesus' sake. Amen.

Concerning Holy Baptism

✠

BLESSED Savior, who after Thy glorious resurrection didst institute Holy Baptism as a covenant of Thy continual grace, I thank Thee that through this Sacrament Thou didst take me in Thine arms and make me Thine own for time and eternity. Grant that I may appreciate more and more this heavenly gift whereby I was made a child of Thy grace. By this holy washing Thou hast bestowed on me the forgiveness of all my sins, the presence of Thy Holy Spirit, and the assurance of eternal life. Let my Baptism be a comfort to me in sorrow, a shield in temptation, a tower of strength in weakness and doubt, a refreshing water on the narrow way to heaven. As Thy faithfulness will not set aside the covenant made with me, grant that I also may remain faithful to Thee unto death and in the end receive the crown of life. Hear me for the sake of Thy love. Amen.

Prayers

PERTAINING TO NATIONAL AFFAIRS

For Peace

✠

LORD God, who hast reconciled the whole world to Thyself through Jesus Christ, our Redeemer, I beseech Thee in Thy divine grace to bring about a better understanding amongst the people of the earth. We all have been redeemed. For each sin-troubled soul there is forgiveness as there is for me.

Open the eyes of those who direct the affairs of the nations to see the folly and wickedness of war. Our transgressions and our indifference toward Thee have sent Thy judgments upon the peoples of the earth. Make us a repentant people who turn with all their heart to Thee and confess Jesus Christ, their Lord and Savior.

We are all of one blood, and for all Thou hast given Thy Son, who has bought on the Cross that peace which passeth all understanding. No matter what race or color we may be, Thou hast redeemed us through Thy Son.

Grant to all Thy believers that they may enjoy national peace wherever they live. Comfort the many families of Thy universal Church who are sorrowing, suffering, hungering. Help them out of their distress, and above all keep them steadfast in the faith. Give them strength and courage to endure amid wars. Establish peace among the peoples of the earth.

Watch today over all Thy faithful children. Keep alive in us the hope of everlasting glory, where all the enemies of Thy Son shall be made His footstool and we live and reign with Him forever and ever. Amen.

On Independence Day

✠

LORD Jesus, King of Kings and Lord of Lords, on this day we are thrilled as we remember the greatness of our country's past and give Thee thanks for the blessings we enjoy through the years. Teach me anew to treasure and appreciate this dearly won liberty of conscience and freedom of worship, which is the very cornerstone of our country's glory. Let me at no time misuse my freedom nor neglect to praise Thy holy name. Help me to appreciate the peace and order maintained by my Government. Give me willingness to share in the processes of this democratic rule; to respect my country's laws, and to work and pray for the preservation of its institutions and serve my country wherever possible. Protect me and my fellow citizens from all subversive opinions, and let not our Government fall a prey to selfish interests. Teach us as a people that Thou art ruling the destinies of men and nations and that the future rests in Thy good counsel. Above all, O Lord, I pray Thee, turn the hearts of the people to that freedom which delivers from sin and death and which Thou alone, Savior and Redeemer, canst give to us all. In Thy name. Amen.

On Independence Day

✠

LORD God, Ruler of the nations, we stand in awe of Thy power, majesty, and judgments. Thou hast placed upon the eternal throne Thy Son, the Lord Jesus Christ, to be King of Kings and Lord of Lords, where He rules with omnipotent power. Oh, grant that at all times we give Him the reverence, honor, and obedience due Him. We thank Thee for Thy guidance in calling into being our country with its orderly form of government and its guarantee of liberty of life and conscience and pursuit of happiness.

With grateful hearts we acknowledge Thy goodness in giving the nation leaders who seek the welfare of the people. Thou didst build and protect the nation. Kindle in our hearts this day a true appreciation of our form of government as an instrument of Thy making. Teach us to share responsibilities and duties of our commonwealth. Protect our courts that at all times they execute justice, that righteousness may prevail and obedience be shown by all. Be Thou our Defender in the years which lie ahead. Ward off all foes threatening our land from without or within. Above all, O heavenly Father, speed the course of Thy Gospel among us, that our people, free in their earthly citizenship, may be liberated from sin, to serve Thee to the glory of Thine eternal name. In Jesus' name we pray. Amen.

On Memorial Day

✠

GRACIOUS Lord, heavenly Father, on this day the minds of men are turned in memory to those who have laid down their lives in defense of our country. We indeed owe a debt of gratitude to them who gave their all that we as a nation may continue our way of life. Grant that we worthily carry on where they have left off that our country may enjoy for generations to come peace and liberty and freedom. May we honor them by bringing the tribute of a ready heart, an obedient life, a worthy citizenship, to our country. Guide the counsels of government. Strengthen the bonds of true loyalty. Let the ideals of liberty and peace prevail. Above all, grant that we, Thy children by faith in Christ, find a field of service in which we, as a salt and leaven, uphold righteousness, order, and peace. In Jesus' name I ask it. Amen.

On Veterans' Day

✠

O LORD, as we remember on this day the horrors of war and the mercies of Thy providence in stemming the destruction of the global hostilities, I plead most earnestly that Thou wouldst preserve peace on earth. And to us guarantee eternal peace with Thee in Christ, and then peace among men. Put into the hearts of the rulers of nations the will to avert bloodshed, strife, and selfishness. Cause men to see the folly of war, and teach them to use the prosperity of peace to establish good will by the spreading of the Gospel, that the foundations of love may be laid through faith in Christ Jesus, the Prince of Peace. In His name I ask it. Amen.

On Labor Day

✠

HEAVENLY Father, Thou art the Foreman and the Giver of our every duty. Teach us to go to our appointed tasks as working for Thee and not as mere men-pleasers. We ask Thee to let Thy Word have free course among all conditions of men that peace and good will may prevail in all places. May Thy grace create in us an undying faith in Thee, and make us willing, one and all, to render a greater service to Thee. Remove all discord and suspicion and dissension, all class conflict and hatred and race prejudice. Give us the necessary ability to render genuine service to Thee and our fellow men. Give us the grace to appreciate one another at work, and quicken our hearts with joy as we perform our daily tasks, mindful that we all are dependent upon one another in human society.

Bless all efforts peaceably to allay strife. Destroy all selfishness, greed, and dishonesty. Give us the grace to repect the rights of others and give credit to whom credit is due. Above all remind us that here we build no enduring city, but are pilgrims and strangers in this world who must one day lay down our tools to appear before Thy judgment throne to give an account to Thee. May we then be found faithful stewards and live in Thy presence forevermore. Amen.

In Days of Unemployment

✠

HEAVENLY Father, I entreat Thine aid and encouragement in these days of unemployment. I beseech Thee to give me a fuller measure of faith in the promises of Thy Word. Grant that I may live trustingly one day at a time, knowing that Thou wilt not fail me. Even the little which I receive I accept with grateful heart. Protect me from the dangers of enforced idleness, unnecessary worry, and sleepless nights. Restore to our community and land normal conditions that we all may find the necessary employment. Root out greed, selfishness, and all other social distress in human society. Grant success, earnestness, sobriety, and skill to those that are employed. Heavenly Father, Thou hast blessed man's labors, and even Thy Son dwelled in a workman's home and toiled in the carpenter shop and hallowed the simple duties of life. I pray Thee, satisfy the hungry with bread, and open Thy hands to give me my daily bread. In Jesus' name. Amen.

For Lawmaking Bodies

✠

HEAVENLY Father, as a citizen of our Commonwealth I intercede with Thee for our representatives in Government. Thou hast established in our midst law-making powers dedicated to the upholding of order and liberty. I beseech Thee, bless and preserve our form of government in State and nation. Grant that our legislators may ever be mindful of the welfare of all their constituents. Grant that they be guided to serve unselfishly the common good of the people. Preserve them from all double-dealing, pettiness, and self-seeking. Protect, I beseech Thee, those liberties of rule by representation which are the cornerstone of our Government. Teach us Christians the grace to use our freedom to proclaim Thy Word and use each and every opportunity to serve our fellow men. May we give proof of our gratitude in seeking the welfare of our State, in using our privileges of ballot and freedom of press and speech for the improvement of our own community and our entire nation. These blessings grant us, dear Lord, for Jesus' sake. Amen.

For the Government

✠

LORD God, as I pray for all who are in authority, I thank Thee especially for our form of government given us in our beloved country. Give me the grace with my fellow citizens to esteem the officers and the magistrates of our Government as sent by Thee. Instill in me that respect and honor which is due to them. I pray Thee, Lord, endow them with wisdom for their several duties, with a spirit of sacrifice for the common welfare, with mercy and justice, with uprightness and kindliness. Correct, I pray Thee, the evils of selfishness, greed, vain desire for honor, or abuse of power in the governments of the world. Grant that the true purposes of government may prevail, safeguarding peace and prosperity, to the end that we may live soberly and uprightly in Thy sight and have opportunity to tell of Thee and Thy kingdom. These petitions I direct to Thee because in Jesus I know Thee as my Father and Lord. Amen.

For Fields and Crops

✠

BEAUTIFUL Savior, King of Creation, we praise Thy power and majesty which Thou hast revealed in the growing things of Thy creation on land and in the sea. Teach me, dear Lord, to know that Thou dost supply, in due season, daily bread for us and all mankind. Banish from my heart all selfishness, all pride. Give us the needed diligence and necessary skill in the sowing and gathering of our harvests. Protect our fields from hail, fire, and floods, and let the earth yield its increase. If it be Thy good will to grant peace and prosperity to the nation, that each one may find sufficient bread for his daily need, quicken our hearts to share with the needy wherever they be. Make us a thankful people as we enjoy working amid growing things, and open our eyes to behold the beauty of Thy creation. Teach us to seek first Thy kingdom and Thy righteousness, and then add the necessary food and protection for today. Grant that the fruits of the field may find their way to those who are most deserving according to Thy grace. These gifts I ask of Thee because Thou art the Giver of all things which we need for body and for soul. Amen.

In a Storm

✠

HEAVENLY Father, I know Thy greatness and my weakness, Thy majesty and my unworthiness. O Lord, I am helpless and need Thy protection. For Jesus' sake abide with me. Test me not beyond my strength in this fearful hour of danger. Protect our homestead (our ship) and my dear ones, especially those who are weak and helpless. Give me faith to cast my anxieties and cares on Thee, who stillest storms and guidest the souls of men through every danger. In Jesus' name. Amen.

At the Time of an Epidemic

✠

HEAVENLY Father, I beseech Thee to turn from me and from my fellow men the destruction and terror of this epidemic. I pray Thee, stay the hand of the Angel of Death as he proceeds from dwelling to dwelling. I ask Thee, above all, to draw me closer to Thee as Thy chastening rod afflicts us. Grief-stricken and fearful, let me not despair of Thy mercies. Grant me the grace in humble repentance and sincere faith to look to Thee, who turnest all things to the good of them that love Thee. Grant the necessary wisdom and success to those who strive to stem the tide of affliction, and quicken our hearts to bear the burdens of one another's grief and need. Lord, in Thy mercy save us. I am mindful of my many shortcomings and transgressions. Blot them out that I may find peace and rest for my soul. Make me sure of my salvation through Thy Word. Then give healing and relief according to Thy good will in Christ Jesus, our Lord and Redeemer. Amen.

At the Threat of War

✠

HUMBLY and contritely, O Lord of heaven and earth, I come before Thee. In anxious dismay I behold the war clouds hanging over our nation and the threatenings of bloodshed and destruction. O Lord, Thou canst even make the wickedness of man to praise Thee and turn to good the sinful plottings of the nations. Yet, heavenly Father, I beseech Thee according to Thy good and gracious will to avert this disaster. Give wisdom and understanding to our leaders that they may find a way to avert war and bloodshed. Remove all bitterness and mass hatred from the hearts of my fellow citizens. Let us all weigh the bitter consequences of war and pray for the peace of the nations. Grant to Thy people in our country that spirit of love and wisdom which will leaven the minds of our nation and turn the hearts of men to peace. Give us Christians the courage to oppose all unnecessary bloodshed and wanton destruction of life. Lord, help! Lord, defend! In Jesus' name. Amen.

At the Outbreak of War

✠

O LORD God Almighty, who from Thy throne dost behold all the nations of the earth, look down with pity upon our country and those nations who are now at war. I confess that, because of our sins, we have deserved Thy chastening; and I pray Thy forgiveness through Jesus Christ, our Lord. I entreat Thee, O God of our salvation, make war to cease, and give peace in our time, that we and all Thy children everywhere may serve Thee with a quiet mind, through Christ Jesus, our Lord. Grant, heavenly Father, that hourly the nation's leaders strive to bring bloodshed to a conclusion. Hold Thy hand over women and children. Check the hatred and cruelty of mankind. Direct the counsels of neighbor nations to overtures of peace. Instill in us all a horror of war and grant us a mighty spirit of prayer to intercede with Thee against all bloodshed and destruction. O Lord, Thou art Master of the world, put an end to these horrors. Bring peace to the people of the earth, and use us to that end. I ask it for Jesus' sake. Amen.

In a National Crisis

✠

KING of Kings and Lord of Lords, Thou Lord of life and death, protect our nation in this great crisis and need. Turn the hearts of men to Thee, and let them find strength and encouragement in Thee and peace of heart and mind through the cleansing in Jesus' blood. Throughout the nation let wise counsel, calm thinking, unselfish aims prevail. With singleness of purpose let one and all support all just measures. In Jesus' name. Amen.

✠

HEAVENLY Father, who hast bidden us to raise up holy hands for all men, I entreat Thee to protect our nation in this present hour of need. Let us not be confounded or dismayed. Give us a staunch heart of loyalty and an earnest spirit of prayer in behalf of all who guide the destiny of the nation. Make even the wickedness of men to praise Thee. Above all, draw us all to Thee with Thy constraining love, and give us a faith that will hold fast to Thee. Amid the tumult of war build Thy kingdom, and turn ever more souls to Thee. So lead us from victory to victory for Jesus' sake. Amen.

In a National Calamity

✠

HEAVENLY Father, I come to Thy throne of mercy, bowed down and wearied by the load of suffering and disaster visited upon our nation. I acknowledge our trespasses before Thee and do not deny my many transgressions of Thy holy Law. We are a sinful nation, laden with iniquity. But there is hope and help in Thee. Thou dost forgive iniquity and sin. Open Thou our eyes to see our evil ways and the need of Thy salvation. Lead us into Thy Word and to Jesus Christ, our only Savior. Grant that we, who are children of Thy grace, may courageously speak to our needy world of the hope which is in our soul, and soothe the hearts of men by the comfort of Thy Gospel. Strengthen the afflicted, lighten the burden of the homeless and the fatherless. Above all, let the fruits of faith flow from our hearts richly in sympathy and mutual care. Enable me to use my opportunities and gifts to Thy glory and others' good. Because of Thy grace we are not altogether lost, but find forgiveness and peace in Thee. O Lord, give me the grace to seek Thee, to trust in Thee, and to confess Thee. In Jesus' name. Amen.

Prayers

FOR VARIOUS OCCASIONS
IN INDIVIDUAL AND FAMILY LIFE

On the Day of a Wedding Anniversary

✠

GRACIOUS and good Lord, today our happy hearts praise Thee as we observe again the anniversary of our wedded bliss. Thy presence in our home and lives has been a benediction which has made us a happy couple. Accept our thanks and the acknowledgments of our hearts as we come before Thee in prayer. We bow to receive from Thy bountiful hands the blessings of Thy grace.

Grant that the years which lie ahead may be enriched with the graces of Thy Holy Spirit, contentment, love, kindness, thoughtfulness and joy.

Keep us steadfast in faith, loyal and devoted to Thee and to each other, consecrating our lives and services to Thy glorious name.

If it be that trials and sorrows come into our lives, be Thou with us with Thy helping and almighty hand that we be not crushed under the load nor doubt Thy power to help.

Today, then, be with us in Thy grace, forgiving our sins and filling our hearts with peace. Grant that the joys of the day be hallowed by Thy gracious approval, through Jesus Christ, our eternal Redeemer. Amen.

Of Husband and Wife

✠

LORD, heavenly Father, Thou hast joined us in holy wedlock that, hand in hand, we walk courageously life's journey in mutual love and oneness of purpose. Bless our home with Thy divine presence, and fill our hearts with an undying devotion to Thee who hast sent Thy Son into the world to hallow every walk of life.

Grant that we may continue day after day to live in Thy grace. Forgive us all our sins, and strengthen our faith in Thy divine grace and mercy. Let Thy Word guide, instruct, and comfort us. Make our hearts temples of Thy Holy Spirit.

As we daily receive Thy divine forgiveness, make us also forgiving toward each other. As Thou art merciful and kind, full of compassion and long-suffering, teach us to be thoughtful, considerate, and patient as we face the problems of the day.

In our joys let us not forget Thee. In our

sorrows let us not despair of Thy help. Protect us as we go in and out of our home. Keep us faithful and steadfast to Thee and Thy Word; through Jesus Christ, our Lord. Amen.

Of a Woman with Child

✠

O GREAT God, heavenly Father, Thou art the Creator and Preserver of life. Marvelous are Thy works. I magnify Thy holy name. Thou hast blessed me. In humility I appear before Thy throne with prayers for my unborn child and myself. Thou, heavenly Counselor and Helper, knowest our needs. Keep from us what might be harmful, and daily bestow on us health and strength. Guide me through Thy Holy Spirit, and let me constantly be mindful of my privilege and my responsibility as a mother. At all times let me place my trust in Thee and Thy fatherly care, knowing that from generation to generation Thy mercy is upon those that lean upon Thee. Grant that, relying on Jesus, my dear Redeemer, and His glorious sacrifice, I may face the future calmly, cheerfully, and in quiet happiness. I ask all this in His name. Amen.

At the Birth of a Child

✠

Wに joy and thanksgiving we come to
Thee, O Lord of Goodness and Love, to praise
Thee out of the fullness of our grateful hearts
that Thou hast gladdened our home and life
with this newborn babe. Our joy is exceedingly
great as Thou hast preserved the mother, who
has gone down into the shadows of death to
bring forth this new life.

We know that this child is a gift of Thy
bountiful hand. Grant us grace and wisdom to
bring up this precious soul in the knowledge
and understanding of Thy Word, which makes
all of us wise unto salvation. As we dedicate
this child to Thee in Holy Baptism, we ask
Thee as its heavenly Father to watch over it
with Thy tenderest care and continued grace.

Bless our child with a healthy body, a clear
mind, and a clean heart, and preserve it to us
according to Thy good and gracious will. Grant
that our child may grow in favor with Thee and
bring sunshine and joy into our hearts and our
home.

Keep us all in Thy grace, forgiving us daily
our sins and filling our souls with peace. Thou

art our Hiding Place. And now to Thee be praise, glory, thanksgiving, for this precious gift this day and forever; through Jesus Christ, who is the Friend of children and the Savior of all. Amen.

At the Baptism of a Child

✠

LORD Jesus, Friend of children, we have brought our child, precious to Thee, to Holy Baptism that it may be Thine now and throughout eternity. Through this blessed Sacrament receive it into Thine everlasting arms of love. Bless and keep it from every danger of body and soul.

By Thy grace develop in this child a healthy body, a clean mind, and nobility of character, faithful to Thee, who hast redeemed it with Thine own precious blood. And at last bring it with us all to the eternal home in heaven to live in Thy presence forevermore. Amen.

At the Baptism of a Child

✠

LORD God eternal, we have dedicated this child to Thee in Holy Baptism, and through this blessed Sacrament Thou hast received it into Thy Kingdom of Grace and made it Thine own, an heir of eternal life. We ask Thee to protect and shield this precious life from all danger of body and soul. Thou knowest how much we love our child. But we also know that Thou lovest it with an even greater love, for Thou hast sent Thy Son into the world to redeem it, that it may be Thine own throughout all eternity.

Lord, Thou knowest all things and canst look down the pathway of this child's life. Guide it into paths of righteousness. Keep it from evil. Preserve it in the saving faith which by Thy Holy Spirit has been placed into its heart through this means of grace. We ask all this in Jesus' name. Amen.

Of a Sponsor

✠

LORD, gracious Father, these Christian parents have asked me to share with them the spiritual care of their newborn child. Grant to me grace that I may always be mindful of my responsibility and be to this child an example of a God-fearing and Christian life. May all I do and say draw it closer to Thee. May it in the years to come love Thy Word, walk in Thy Commandments, obey Thy will, and find joy in Thy Gospel. Preserve this precious soul in the only-saving faith, which is in Christ Jesus, our Lord. Guard it from sin and temptations. Keep it healthy in body and mind. Grant, merciful Lord, that I do nothing to offend it. Wherever I have sinned against Thee, forgive, and keep me likewise faithful to Thy Word to the end. I ask it in Jesus' name. Amen.

Of Parents

✠

GRACIOUS Lord, Thou hast entrusted to us this precious soul which has been redeemed through Jesus Christ our Lord, that we may bring it up in Thy Church here on earth that it may be Thine in the glories of eternal life forevermore. Grant that we may earnestly strive to follow the instructions of Thy Word and train our child to know the Scriptures and to love Thee and Thy Son, Jesus Christ, our Lord.

Give grace that this child may grow up with a healthy body, a believing heart, and an obedient mind, loving Thy Gospel and walking in the ways of righteousness.

We know, O Lord, that ours is not an easy task. Give us grace and strength to perform our duties as Christian parents and be an example in word and act in our home and in our daily life.

Make us a praying people who are mindful of Thy presence. May our hearts be temples of Thy Holy Spirit and our home a forecourt of heaven. Protect us all from bodily harm, and preserve our souls from the onslaughts of Satan and sin. May we continually grow in grace and knowledge of Thee and Thy Word and finally one and all live in the glories of heaven to praise Thee, world without end. We ask this for the sake of Jesus Christ, the Friend of children and the Savior of us all. Amen.

Of Children

✠

LORD Jesus, who of old didst bless the children brought to Thee, bless us also, who by our loving parents have been dedicated to Thee in our Baptism. Keep us faithful, steadfast, and loyal to Thee. Teach us to do Thy will and follow graciously Thy Word. Lord Jesus, grant us strength to do those things that become Christian children living in Christian homes. Give us grace that we may be obedient to the kindly instructions of our parents.

Bless Father and Mother; preserve them to us for many years to come. We thank Thee that Thou hast given us parents who provide for the needs of our body and soul. Make us appreciative of our Christian home and the Christian training we are receiving. May we find joy in the reading and studying of Thy Word and grow steadily in knowledge of Thy saving Gospel.

Protect us as we go in and out of this home, and bring Father safely home each evening of the week. We ask all this in Jesus' name. Amen.

For an Erring Child

✠

LORD Jesus, who hast come into the world to seek and to save those that are lost, with heavy and bleeding hearts we come to Thee, the Friend of sinners, imploring Thee to save our erring child. O Lord, our hearts are breaking as we realize that this our son (daughter) is going the way of transgressors, which leads to destruction. Save him (her), O Lord, save him (her). Thou canst in Thy mercy perform wonders and find a way to bring back the erring who have wandered away from Thy fold.

O Lord, if by any fault or neglect of mine he (she) has strayed from Thee, forgive me. Show me a way to undo my mistakes.

Draw us all closer to Thee. Let him (her) who is lost be found that our hearts be filled again with peace and joy. Unite our family in Thee and abide in our hearts now and forevermore as the loving, compassionate, and forgiving Savior. Amen.

Upon Occupying a New Home

✠

O LORD, as we enter into our new home, come Thou with us, and let Thy divine presence bless us with the riches of Thy grace as we go in and out. Grant that we may keep out of this home all selfishness, pride, thoughtlessness. Preserve us from all irritating and petty worries. Let Thy Word dwell here abundantly. Teach us day by day to be forgiving as we are forgiven of Thee.

Strengthen our faith that we may be able to withstand the assaults of Satan. Keep us faithful to Thy Church and to the glorious Gospel, which tells us that we are reconciled to Thee through Christ Jesus, our Lord.

Bless the labors of our hands, and grant that all we say and do may glorify Thy wonderful name. Preserve us from want and sickness, anxious cares, and fretful worries. Let Thy peace dwell in our hearts and lives.

Bring to our home many Christian friends. Grant that in all our joys and festivities, gatherings and entertainments, we may so conduct ourselves that we do not give offense to the church nor the world. Make this home a forecourt of heaven and our hearts temples wherein Thou dwellest. Let Thy Word abide with us day after day. Forgive us each and every sin, and bring us at last to Thine eternal home in heaven; through Jesus Christ, our Lord. Amen.

For the Home

✠

LORD Jesus, abide with us. Make this home a dwelling place of Thy continual presence, and keep us faithful to Thee and Thy Word. Let the joy of the Gospel dwell in our hearts. Let our daily conversations be hallowed and pleasing and acceptable to Thee. Preserve us from sin. Be with us in the hour of temptation. Keep us unworried and untroubled. Remove from our lives all unbelief and indifference. Strengthen our faith, deepen our love to Thee, and make us a consecrated people who day after day commune with Thee in prayer.

Pour out upon us Thy saving grace as we come daily with our sins, our needs, our sorrows, and our troubles to Thee. Be with us as we face the hardships of life, and give us those things which we need, for both body and soul, for our home and our family.

Grant that daily Thy Word may purify our souls, strengthen our faith, make us obedient to Thy will. As Thou art patient and forgiving with us, make us forgiving, thoughtful, kind, and considerate one toward another.

As we go in and out of this home, bless us, and grant us at last a home with Thee in glory. Amen.

For the Home

✠

In sincere gratitude, O Lord, we bow our heads and hearts to worship Thee and give thanks to Thee for all the mercies Thou hast shown to us this day. Thou hast protected each and every one and brought us into our family circle healthy in body and mind. To Thee, the eternal Keeper of our lives, we come to acknowledge Thy goodness and love. Continue to bless this home, and hold each one of us in the hollow of Thy hand.

Forgive us all our sins. Fill our hearts with a love for Thee and for one another, that peace and harmony may continue to fill this household. Let no place be dearer to us than our Christian home, and let Thy Word dwell in our midst. Protect us all and grant that none of us err or stray from Thee or do anything to disgrace our family before Thee or the world. Keep us faithful to Thy Gospel and true to one another, and finally let us all reach the eternal home of all Thy children. We ask this in Jesus' name. Amen.

For Those Away from Home

✠

LORD, gracious and merciful, who watchest even over the sparrows on the housetops and dost uphold all things with Thine everlasting arms, protect and keep our loved ones while they are away from home. Watch Thou over them tenderly that no evil come nigh to them and us as we are separated one from another.

Keep them faithful to Thy Word and Thy Church. Guard and protect them as they are tempted by the allurements of sin and the unbelief of the world.

Keep them pure in heart and clean in mind and healthy in body. Dwell in them day by day. Abide with us and with them, and bring them safely home to us and at last to the eternal home in heaven. Then Thine shall be the glory, Thine the praise, world without end; through Jesus Christ, our Lord. Amen.

While Away from Home

✠

O LORD, who art present everywhere, be very near to those at home, and protect them from every danger of body and soul.

Heavenly Father, I thank Thee for the comforting promises which Thou hast given in Thy Word to me and to all Thy children. Thou art our Hiding Place and our Refuge, a very present Help in every situation of life. As the eternal Caretaker Thou dost not slumber nor sleep. Grant that this promise may give me the needed spiritual security. Turn Thou, as gracious Lord, all things to the good of those that love Thee. Therefore guide and direct all things in our lives and home to our eternal welfare.

Increase in us a greater love of Thee. Thou hast made a covenant with us in our Baptism by which Thou art our heavenly Father, and we children of Thy grace. I know that Thou never dost break Thy covenant with us. Give grace that we, too, may be faithful to this baptismal agreement. I confess that we have not always loved Thee with all our heart, yet in Thy mercy Thou didst not turn from us. O compassionate Lord, forgive each and every one of us all our sins today, and protect us, as we are apart, during this coming night. Unite us with Thee in our common prayers, and bring me safely home. In Jesus' name I ask this. Amen.

For a Member of the Family in Danger

✠

O GOD, my ever-present Help in trouble, I beseech Thee to be with me in this hour of great danger and distress. Keep me calm, composed, confident, trustful. Thou art with me. See me through this trying hour. Let me not doubt that Thou canst help to the uttermost. O Lord, I put all my trust in Thee.

Thy will be done, O God. Let it be a gracious will. Grant me strength to believe that all is well for time and eternity. Today I look through a glass, darkly, but around Thy throne there is no darkness at all. Even in these anxious moments I praise Thee, because I put all my trust in Thee.

O Lord, uphold me. Do not forsake me. Look upon me in mercy, and forgive me my sins. Strengthen my faith. Give me courage.

Bring peace to my soul. Protect my loved ones, and, above all, preserve us all in Thy grace now and forevermore, for the sake of our Redeemer, Christ Jesus, our Lord. Amen.

In Times of Illness in the Family

✠

O LORD, eternal God, who art our Father in Christ Jesus, hear our prayer as we come to Thee in our trouble and distress. Thou art our Hiding Place. We have no other refuge in an hour like this. Gracious Lord, Thou canst heal. Thy grace can restore to health and give us strength to carry on. We know that Thou art merciful and gracious, for Thou hast sent Christ to the Cross to redeem us and make us Thine own. Surely Thou wilt not forsake us in this hour of suffering and pain.

O Lord, we confess that we have not always given Thee the first place in our lives; forgive us. Today blot out all our sins through Christ's precious blood. Remove the worries and anxious fears which want to beset us. Give us grace to trust in Thee who art our loving Father in Christ Jesus, our Lord. Amen.

WITH GOD

Begin the day with God:
   Kneel down to Him in prayer;
Lift up thy heart to His abode
   And seek His love to share.

Open the Book of God,
   And read a portion there;
That it may hallow all thy thoughts
   And sweeten all thy care.

Go through the day with God,
   Whate'er thy work may be;
Where'er thou art—at home, abroad,
   He still is near to thee.

Conclude the day with God:
   Thy sins to Him confess;
Trust in the Lord's atoning blood,
   And plead His righteousness.

Lie down at night with God,
   Who gives His servants sleep.
And when thou tread'st the vale of death
   He will thee guard and keep.

              —Author Unknown

BENEDICTION

The Lord bless us and keep us.
The Lord make His face to shine upon
  us and be gracious unto us.
The Lord lift up His countenance upon
  us and give us peace.

                    Amen

Of One Who Is Ill

✠

LORD, with my anxious cares and troubles I come to Thee, trusting in Thy holy Word and believing in Thy promises. Thou knowest that I have been greatly upset by the worries, fears, and doubts of the day. Thou must be my Strength and Refuge if I am to find peace of mind and healing for my body. Uphold me with Thine almighty arm.

I am not worthy of Thy love and mercy, for I have sinned and often done evil in Thy sight. Blot out all my transgressions through Christ's precious blood. Fill my soul with peace. Give me the grace to put all my trust in Thee. Let Thy healing hand rest upon me day after day. Enable me by Thy grace to rise above all my suffering to praise Thee, whose will is wiser than mine own. Keep me and this household in Thy saving grace, and abide with us all the days of our life; through Jesus Christ, our Lord. Amen.

Of One Who Is Ill

✠

LORD Jesus, Strength of the weary and a very present Help to all who are in distress, I come to Thee with my many burdens and sins. Cleanse my soul, O Lord, and heal my body. Safely see me through the troubled waters of the day. Remove all sinful thoughts and worries from my heart, and let me find peace in Thee. Lead me again to Calvary to behold Thy boundless love, O gracious Savior. Fill my soul with the joy of forgiveness and the hope of everlasting life. Let not the sufferings and the cares of this day make me despondent. Teach me to believe that Thy abiding presence will uphold me from hour to hour. Give to me peaceful days and restful nights. Bless me with a refreshing sleep. Come to me with healing in Thy wings. Speak to my soul the comforting promises of Thy Word, and keep me steadfast in the faith to the end. Bless this household, and keep all of us cheerful, hopeful, and confident. I ask this of Thee, who hast redeemed me with Thine own blood. Amen.

Of One Who Is Ill

✠

DIVINE Lord, Thou hast been gracious and merciful to me in Christ Jesus. Forgive me all my sins day after day. Accept my thanks for this Thy goodness. Let me find my joy in Thee, who hast brought to my heart salvation and peace.

In Thy mercy look upon my distress and pain, and forgive me all my sins and all my worryings. Ease Thou my suffering, and make me patient and cheerful in my affliction. Bless those who take care of me. Let them not become weary in this service which they must render to me. Keep us faithful to Thy Word, and grant that we may continue in Thy grace until life's journey ends and we behold Thee in the glory of eternity, through Jesus Christ, our Lord. Amen.

Of One Who Is Ill

✠

DIVINE Savior, Shepherd of our souls, embrace me with Thy love, and protect me throughout this day. I need Thee, for I am wounded and bruised, sick at heart and in trouble and distress. To Thee I come. Forgive me all my sins in Thy mercy and love, and uphold me amid these trials and tribulations. Strengthen my faith. Take every doubt out of my heart, and lead me into Thy Word, where Thou dost promise to be with me always in every situation of life. Calm my nerves. Put my mind at ease. Make me hopeful and patient. O Christ, have mercy upon me. O Christ, be Thou with me now and forevermore. Amen.

Before an Operation

✠

HEAVENLY Father, in this hour of anxiety I come to Thee pleading for Thy divine presence and aid. As the time of the operation draws near, I need a staff on which to lean. To whom shall I turn but to Thee, gracious Lord? Thou hast created, redeemed, and sanctified me. Thou wilt not forsake Thy child crying to Thee for help and strength in trouble and pain. I confess to Thee my unworthiness, my many weaknesses, shortcomings, and transgressions. Mercifully forgive me for the sake of the sacrifice of Thy dear Son, my precious Savior. Give wisdom and understanding to physicians and nurses that all they do will bring about a speedy recovery in keeping with Thy good, fatherly will. I commend myself into Thy hands. While I slumber and sleep, watch Thou over me. Comfort me with the assurance of my salvation through the precious blood of Thy Son Jesus Christ. Grant me a faith which will not falter nor fail in the present hour. Take every fear out of my heart. Thy name I praise, O Lord of life and death. Hear my prayer for the sake of Thy dear Son. Amen.

After an Operation

✠

BLESS the Lord, O my soul, and, all that is within me, bless His holy name. O merciful Father in heaven, Thou hast fulfilled Thy promises upon me and been with me in the hour of anxiety and pain. When I was weak and helpless, Thou hast been my Strength. I called upon Thee in my trouble; Thou didst deliver me. Now I glorify Thee. Thou didst bless the surgeon with skill and safely hast brought me through this operation. Thou didst not count my sins against me, but hast graciously forgiven them for Christ's sake. O gracious Father, continue the favors Thou hast bestowed upon me, and if it be Thy will, grant me full and speedy recovery. Bless me with a restful day and a refreshing sleep this night. As Thou watchest over me in these trying days, grant me patience, and let my thoughts dwell on Thy goodness. Thou art my Shepherd; make me confident that I shall not want. O gracious Father, I cast all my cares upon Thee, for Thou carest for me. Hear my prayer for the sake of Jesus Christ, my adorable Savior. Amen.

Of a Convalescent

✠

LORD God, my heavenly Father, when Thy chastening was upon me, I poured out my prayer to Thee; when I was in sore distress, I called upon Thy holy name. Thou, my God and Father, hast graciously inclined Thine ears to the cries of Thy troubled child. Thou hast mercifully heard my supplication and the fervent prayers of my friends and relatives. I have experienced the fulfillment of Thy age-old promise: I am the Lord that healeth thee. Thy sweet Gospel was brought to me by my pastor and my fellow Christians and comforted and quieted my weary, fainting soul with the assurance of

Thy grace and forgiveness in Christ, my Savior. Thy loving wisdom blessed the skill and kind attention of physicians and nurses that I now am recovering. Not to us, O Lord, not to us, but to Thy name I give glory for Thy mercy and for Thy truth's sake. In heartfelt gratitude I present myself, body and soul, a living thank-offering to Thee, my Father, my Redeemer, my Comforter. Keep me steadfast in faith, in love, in hope, and receive me at last into Thy heavenly mansions for the sake of the healing, justifying, sanctifying blood of Thy Son, Christ Jesus. Amen.

Of a Convalescent

✠

LORD Jesus, as my thoughts go back to the days of my anguish and pain, I gratefully remember Thy gracious presence and merciful aid during the days of my sickness. Give me the grace to fulfill the many vows and pledges which rose from my heart to Thy throne of mercy while I lay on my bed of grief and suffering. Lord, let me not in the days of health forget the promises made in the days of my tribulation and sorrow. Thou didst not forsake me in my misfortune, let me never turn from Thee, neither in life nor in death. In days of joy let Thy Word and the fulfillment of Thy will be the joy and rejoicing to my heart. In days of sorrow let me prove that I have learned the lesson well taught me in these hours of trial, that tribulation worketh patience; and patience, experience; and experience, hope; and hope maketh not ashamed; because Thy love, O God, is shed abroad in my heart by the Holy Spirit. Teach me to say at all times: Thy will, not mine, be done, in full assurance that all things work together for good to me and that no creature, no man, nor devil, can pluck me out of Thy hands, who art my Father in Jesus Christ, my Savior. Amen.

At the Approach of Death

✠

O LORD, Thou knowest how much we love him (her) who is sick unto death, but Thy love is still greater, for Thou hast redeemed him (her) with the precious blood of Thine own Son. If it be Thy will that he (she) should pass out of this mortal life, receive him (her) to Thyself in glory. If this be his (her) last night on earth, let Thy holy angels take him (her) into Thy presence, where there is no more pain and suffering and sin, but fullness of joy forevermore. Wash him (her) of all sin, and accept him (her) for Jesus' sake. Strengthen our faith, and keep us close to Thee. In Jesus' name we ask it. Amen.

After a Death

✠

AMID our tears, O Lord, we praise Thee as Thou hast received our loved one to Thyself in glory for all eternity. We thank Thee that Thou hast brought him (her) to the knowledge of Jesus Christ, our Lord and Savior. Comfort us with the glorious hope of the resurrection and the life eternal. Grant us grace to say with a believing heart: "Thy will be done," and to know that Thy will is a good and gracious will even in the present hour. Comfort us through Thy Gospel, which promises strength and help to the troubled and weary. O Lord, forsake us not in this hour; for Jesus' sake we ask it. Amen.

Of Mourners

✠

O LORD, our hearts are heavy with sorrow. Thy ways are certainly not our ways. Yet we want to believe that Thou art not forsaking us. O Lord, Thou art trying us as in the refiner's fire, yet we believe that Thou dost love us with an everlasting love.

Thou alone canst pour healing into our sorrowing and wounded hearts. Lord, we do not murmur. But Thou knowest how empty and lonely life has become for us. We do not begrudge our loved one the glory which Thou hast promised to Thy faithful people; but, Lord, we do miss him (her). Life is so dreary, and the hours are filled with sorrow and grief. However, amid our tears we thank Thee that Thou hast brought him (her) to the knowledge of Jesus Christ as his (her) Savior. We thank Thee that he (she) has departed in peace, reconciled to Thee through Christ's precious blood. We praise Thee that by Thy boundless grace there is no condemnation for those who believe. Through his (her) departure teach us to know and realize that here we have no abiding city and that the foundation for our eternal home has been laid in heaven. Keep us faithful to Thy saving Word, that we, too, may depart in peace when life's journey ends, washed clean in the blood of our precious Savior, to enter into glory, there to live with our loved ones in the Savior's presence eternally. O Lord, abide with us, for Jesus' sake. Amen.

Of a Mourner

✠

O LORD, if it were not for the promise of the resurrection and life eternal, I could not endure this sorrow which has befallen me. Only the assurance of Thy continual presence has enabled me to carry on during these lonely months. Only Thy grace has preserved in me this faith which comforts me in an hour like this. O Lord, do not let me mourn as those that have no hope.

Thou hast taken care of me in Thy mercy and goodness. In Thy loving-kindness Thou hast provided for my needs. Thou hast been guiding me from day to day. O Lord, I thank Thee for these mercies. Open to my heart the glories of heaven, and fill me with the precious hope of eternal life which makes me untroubled and unafraid. Protect me against every danger of body and soul. Comfort me day after day with the precious promises of Thy Word. Give me grace to come to Thee and find rest for my soul. Forgive me all my sins. I ask this in Jesus' name. Amen.

On One's Birthday

✠

GRACIOUS Lord, Thou hast brought me to the threshold of another year. The year has been rich in blessings coming from Thy bountiful hand of love. Day after day Thou hast protected me and safely seen me through the many trials and temptations of life. I am not worthy of all this goodness and grace. Often have I sinned against Thee and offended Thee with my many transgressions. Forgive me, Lord, for Jesus' sake. Let me start life anew, led by Thee throughout this coming year.

O Lord, keep me in Thy love. Give me the grace to dedicate myself, my entire life, to Thee. Let my greatest joy be found in Thy Word and in doing Thy will.

Heavenly Father, I am sinful and unworthy, yet I come because Thou rememberest that I am dust. Abide with me day by day. Put Thy protecting arm around me, and keep me steadfast in faith, that my days may glorify Thee who hast called me into the kingdom of Thy dear Son, Jesus Christ, my Lord and Savior. Amen.

Of Those Engaged

✠

O LORD, my heart leaps with joy. My day is filled with gladness because Thou hast brought to me one in whom I have found a partner of life. Lord, I thank and praise Thee who hast led our paths toward each other. I know that Thou dost guide the footsteps of all who are Thine own.

And now, gracious Lord, grant that we as engaged people will so live and act that we do not give offense to our fellow men nor lose our respect for each other. Lord, be Thou with us as the unseen Friend and mutual Lover. May we ever remember that we first of all belong to Thee.

Guard us fom jealousy, envy, misunderstandings, and deepen our love for each other.

Make our hearts Thy temple. Keep us standing in Thy grace. Keep us pure and clean within, and let us glorify Thy name through our conduct and life. Bless us, O Lord, and our families. I ask this in Jesus' name. Amen.

Of One in Love

✠

O LORD, who dost direct our lives day after day, I thank Thee that Thou hast so graciously led me through these days of my youth and hast preserved me from straying and falling. I come to Thee for special guidance in these days when I am choosing a life companion. Lord, Thou canst look down the pathway of my life. Thou knowest if this young woman (man) is truly a fitting partner and companion for me. If so, O Lord, grant that our lives may be fused into one and we journey on together happily.

Keep me pure in heart. Grant that I may do nothing to offend Thee. Grant that my conduct may bespeak my Christian faith.

O Lord, if it be Thy will, grant I beseech Thee, that we two may understand each other better from day to day and love each other sin-

cerely. Above all, give us the grace to keep
Thee in our hearts as our Friend and Guide.
I ask this for the sake of Jesus, my Lord and
Savior. Amen.

Of a Young Person

✠

GIVE ear to my words, O my Savior;
hearken to the voice of my cry, my King and
my God, for to Thee will I pray. Thy perfect
righteousness has atoned for my many failings,
sins, and iniquities. Trusting in Thy grace, I pray
Thee, precious Savior, remember not the sins
of my youth nor my many transgressions. Blot
out all my follies and shortcomings with Thy
holy, precious blood, shed for me on the Cross
of Calvary. Enable me, O Thou Fountain of
strength, to make the perfection of Thy life the
constant pattern of my life and conversation.
Help me to flee youthful lusts, wicked compan-
ionships, and whatever entices my sinful flesh.
Grant that I may at all times follow after righteousness, godliness, faith, love, patience, meekness. Let Thy holy Word be my constant guide
and source of strength. May the Holy Spirit lead
me wherever I go, that I may never stray from
the path which Thou hast chosen for me. In a

perishing world let me be a salt and a light; teach me to perform gladly my duties as a member of Thy Church and a citizen of the country. Keep me and my loved ones from all evil. Preserve my going out and my coming in from this time forth and even forevermore, my mighty Redeemer. Amen.

Of a Businessman

✠

LORD, Thou hast prospered the labor of my hands and hast given success to my endeavors. Kind and gracious Father, grant to me an ever grateful heart, that I may never forget all Thy mercies and all the truth which Thou hast shown Thy servant, unworthy though I be. Help me to accept humbly the responsibilities and obligations which success has placed upon me. Indelibly impress upon me the need of trusting in Thee, the living God, and in Thy Son, my only Savior, and not in the unstable riches of this present day, which tomorrow can be shaken out of my hands. Teach me, O God of love, to be rich in good works, always ready to come to the aid of my brethren, ever willing to give and share according to my ability in the building up and extension of Thy kingdom at home and abroad. Help me by the power of Thy Holy Spirit to lay up in store for myself a good foundation against the time to come, that through the faith of my Redeemer I may lay hold on eternal life, which He has procured on the Cross of redemption for me and all mankind. Amen.

In Business Reverses

✠

THE Lord gave, and the Lord hath taken away; blessed be the name of the Lord. O my heavenly Father, I, Thy poor, harassed child, come to Thee for comfort, for peace of mind, for guidance, and for aid. Thou knowest even better than I the worries and anxious forebodings which are troubling my heart and mind. Whither shall I flee in my distress but to Thee, my gracious, omnipotent Father? Enable me to humble myself under Thy almighty hand and cast all my cares upon Thee, who carest for me. I know that even these business reverses are sent as a needed chastening for my eternal welfare. Heavenly Father, for the sake of Thy Son, my Redeemer, forgive me all my sins. Let these losses teach me to know the uncertainty and vanity of all earthly riches. Create in me that godliness and contentment which is great gain. In accordance with Thy gracious will, let me again succeed and prosper. If not, O Lord, let me at least become richer in faith and good works. Supply me each day with the necessary food, and grant me the grace to live trustingly, and remain Thy loving, trustful child, kissing the rod wherewith Thou art chastening me. May I firmly cling to the word of Thy promise: Fear not, for I will never leave thee nor forsake thee. Thy will be done, O my heavenly Father! Hear me for Jesus' sake. Amen.

During Hard Times

✠

O LORD, we are sorely tried in these days of want and need, yet we are trusting in Thee. Thou hast promised to open Thy hand to satisfy the hunger of every living creature. Feed us, O Lord.

We know that our sins and the sinfulness of mankind have brought on these trying days. Forgive us, O Lord, all our sins, our neglects, our indifference, our coldness. We have not always loved Thee with all our heart nor served Thee with all our strength. O Lord, we confess that we have not given Thee of Thine own in the days when Thou hast blessed us. We have been unfaithful stewards. Have mercy upon us, and visit us again with Thy grace and love, and break to us our daily bread.

O Lord, in Thy mercy turn again Thy face toward us. We come with repentant hearts; receive us. We come hungry; supply our needs. We have none other to whom we can go. Thou great God, help us, and give us today that which we need to sustain our body and life. Fill our souls with peace, forgiving us all our sins. Take from us all anxious thoughts and worries of today. Then Thine shall be the glory now and forever; through Jesus Christ, our Lord. Amen.

In Days of Personal Unemployment

✠

O GOD, Thou hast been my Help in the days which lie in the past. Turn not from me in the present hour as I walk the streets, discouraged and disheartened, seeking work. Surely Thou dost care for me. Guide me with Thine eye. Lead and direct me to find suitable employment.

O Lord, my sins are ever before me. In my

yesterdays I have not always served Thee. Too often I have ignored Thy goodness and Thy mercy. Forgive me, and let me find peace for my soul in Thee.

Take all resentment, bitterness, and rebellion out of my heart. Make me hopeful, cheerful, courageous, patient, and confident.

Thou hast promised to be with me in the day of trouble. Open Thine hands and satisfy my needs. Teach me to face the day confident of Thy goodness. O Lord, let me not doubt Thy promises. Hear the cry of my distressed heart and disturbed mind. Have mercy upon me, for Jesus' sake. Amen.

In Behalf of the Unemployed

✠

DIVINE Lord, gracious and full of tender mercies, look upon the many breadwinners who are without work and without food, anxious, worried, troubled, and distressed. They are in want in our land of plenty.

I confess that all this has come upon us because of our sins. We have ignored Thee, O Lord. We have served other interests in place of serving Thee. We have not made Thee our All in all. As a nation we have largely forgotten

Thee and ignored Thy Gospel call. Many have desecrated the day set aside to worship Thee. We have not fed upon Thy Word, but upon the husks and ashes of pleasure, yea, often upon sinful enjoyments.

Thou hast not failed to open Thine hands, but our selfishness has withheld the daily food from many.

Cause us all to turn to Thee with repentant hearts. Grant that we be more considerate and thoughtful of one another. Those who are without work draw to Thyself with the cords of Thy constraining love. Let them not become despondent or embittered, but see in all these things the wholesome chastenings of a loving Father. Feed all little children. Open our hearts with a sympathetic and understanding love toward all. I ask this in the name of our compassionate Savior, Jesus, our Lord. Amen.

For an Aviator

✠

ETERNAL Lord, who makest the winds and clouds obey Thy will and protectest the eagle in his flight and the dove seeking safety, uphold me as I soar into the sky and fly above land and sea. Pilot my ship safely through the air, and give me nerves which are steady and relaxed, a mind, calm and composed, as I sail on to my destination. Give me a successful take-off and at journeys' end a safe landing, that no harm come to me and those entrusted to my care.

Hold Thy protecting hand over me as I pass through storm and clouds — and let me not lose my way as I fly by instrument through fog and darkness.

Above all, keep me in Thy grace and favor for Jesus' sake, and let my last landing bring me safely into Thy presence, redeemed and saved to praise Thee eternally and forever. Amen.

A Soldier's Prayer

✠

DEAR Father in heaven, I, Thy child, come to Thee, asking for Thy divine protection and gracious guidance while I am in the service of my country. By the precious blood of Thy Son Thou hast bought me as Thine own. In Thy Word Thou hast given me the assurance that the very hairs of my head are all numbered. Trusting in Thy promise and relying upon Thy grace, I confidently ask Thee to protect me against all danger and deliver me from all evil of body and soul.

O Jesus, my Redeemer, let me never forget at what cost Thou hast redeemed me. May the memory of Thy bitter suffering and death keep me from sin and wickedness, indifference to Thy mercy, and coldness of heart. Wash me daily in Thy precious blood. Cleanse me from all my transgressions and iniquities, and by Thy grace enable me to follow in Thy footsteps and do Thy will.

O Holy Spirit, strengthen me in the hour of temptation. Keep me pure in heart, and chaste in body, obedient to my superiors, considerate of all my fellow soldiers, a living example of true Christian faith.

O God of my salvation, let me be and remain Thine own in time and eternity for Jesus' sake. Amen.

A Sailor's Prayer

✠

Lord Jesus, Thy almighty hand has made the earth and sky and sea. Thou art the omnipotent Ruler of the mighty waters of the deep. Wherever my duties in the service of my country may take me, even though it be to the uttermost part of the sea, I know that even there Thy hand shall lead me, and Thy right hand shall uphold me. Those hands were extended on the Cross for my salvation, the hands on which Thou hast graven me with love, the hands out of which no power of earth and hell shall pluck me. Precious Jesus, be Thou at all times my mighty Protector, my gracious Guide, my very present Help in every trouble. Preserve and strengthen me in my faith, that I may at all times trust in Thy atoning blood. Keep me pure and humble, loyal and courageous, in the service of my country. Grant that I accept tasks assigned to me without complaint. In dangerous storms hold Thy guarding hand over our ship and our entire crew. Dispel all fear and terror. Thou art mightier than the mightiest waves and canst protect Thy children in the raging winds and the treacherous billows. May Thy peace keep my whole spirit, that my soul and body be preserved blameless to the great day of Thy coming, my Redeemer and Lord. Amen.

Of a Student of Theology

✠

O THOU eternal God, Father, Son, and Holy Spirit, by Thy unmerited grace I have been permitted to prepare for Thy service in the holy ministry, the office of preaching Thy Word for the salvation of mankind. Give me a grateful heart which may never forget Thy boundless loving-kindness nor the many sacrifices which my parents and Christian friends make to enable me to pursue my studies. Make me a diligent and conscientious student. Grant that I pass not by a single opportunity to gain a better knowledge of all things pertaining to my future calling. May my greatest delight be found in Thy Word, which brings salvation to my soul and rejoicing to my heart. In my study hours be Thou at my side, and keep all disturbing thoughts from my mind. Let me experience the quickening power of Thy Holy Spirit. Lead me ever deeper into all revealed truth, that I may become a faithful servant, approved of Thee, a workman that needeth not to be ashamed. Bless Thou me, O bounteous Fountain of wisdom, and make me a blessing to many. Amen.

Of a Student of Theology

FOR SINCERITY

✠

O THOU faithful God, who hast called me through Thy holy Word into the fellowship of Thy Son Jesus Christ, my Lord and Savior, I pray Thee preserve in me a steadfast and unwavering faith in Thy Word of truth, to the end that I may be found blameless in the day of our Lord Jesus Christ. Keep me, I ask Thee, through Thy Holy Spirit from hypocrisy and insincerity, and make my whole being pure and faithful and sincere in every word and act. Let me see in Thy Word not the wisdom of man, but Thy revelation, given to make me wise unto salvation. Grant that Thy Holy Spirit fill my heart and mind with devout meditation as I read Thy Word and then apply it to the need of my own heart and life. Grant that all my prayers may be sincere, rising from a heart that is dedicated to Thee. May my words and actions ever reveal that I belong to Jesus, who has purchased me with His own blood. Let me be an example to all in word, in conversation, in charity, in spirit, in faith, in purity. Sanctify me wholly, O Thou God of peace, that my whole spirit and soul and body be preserved blameless unto the coming of my Lord and Savior Jesus Christ. Amen.

For Stronger Faith

✠

LORD, I believe. Help Thou mine unbelief! Strengthen Thou my weak and flickering faith. I know that Thou art my gracious Father for Jesus' sake and hast made Christ to me Wisdom and Righteousness and Sanctification and Redemption. Lord, strengthen this faith in me that I may never fear nor faint in any trial or temptation. Though my faith be tried with fire, may I ever be found strong and unmovable to the glory of Thy holy name, who art the Author and Finisher of my faith. Let me firmly believe that the blood of Jesus Christ cleanses me from all sin, that though my sins be as scarlet, they shall be as white as snow, though they be red like crimson, they shall be as wool. When enticed by sin and the world beckons, and my own passions want to yield, help Thou mine unbelief, and give me the power and will to resist. When trials, sorrow, and affliction want to rob me of this trust in Thee, O Lord, help me to conquer and win new victories. Strengthen Thou my faith in Thy promise that all things must work together for good to them that love God, to them that are called according to Thy purpose to be Thine own in time and eternity. Thou, O almighty Lord, canst help; Thou, O gracious Lord, wilt help mine unbelief. Thou canst, Thou wilt, strengthen my faith. Lord, I believe! Amen.

For a Sanctified Life

✠

LORD Jesus, Thou hast redeemed me by Thy blood and called me as Thine own, a fellow citizen with the saints, a member of the household of God. Lord, Thou knowest all things, Thou knowest that I love Thee. Thou knowest that my renewed heart desires to serve Thee in perfect righteousness and holiness, lay aside every weight, cast away the sin that so easily besets me, and run with patience the race that is set before me. Alas, how often have I failed to do what Thou, my precious Savior, hast asked of me. How often have I refused to follow Thee and Thy example! Instead, I have chosen the paths of the world and the desires of my sinful passions. I know that in me, that is, in my flesh, dwelleth no good thing. The good that I would, I do not; but the evil which I would not, that I do. O wretched man that I am! Who shall deliver me from the body of this death? To Thee, Lord Jesus, my Savior and my compassionate Friend, I flee. Help me, or else I perish! Thou Author and Finisher of my faith, Thou hast delivered me from the guilt and the punishment of sin, Thou hast redeemed me also from its power and dominion. Cleanse me and sanctify me wholly. Purge every evil desire and thought out of my heart and mind. Fill me with a pure and perfect love of Thee that I may do Thy will. Whether I live or die, let me be Thine alone and forever, Lord Jesus. Amen.

Prayers at Table

✠

Before the Meal

Come, Lord Jesus, be our Guest,
And let Thy gifts to us be blessed. Amen.

✠

Lord God, Heavenly Father, who so graciously hast opened Thy hands to supply us with daily bread, in sincere appreciation we acknowledge Thy bountiful goodness and love in Christ Jesus, our Lord. Amen.

✠

The eyes of all wait upon Thee, O Lord, and Thou givest them their meat in due season; Thou openest Thine hand and satisfiest the desire of every living thing. Amen.

✠

Lord God, Heavenly Father, bless us and these Thy gifts, which we receive from Thy bountiful goodness, through Jesus Christ, our Lord. Amen.

After the Meal

We give thanks to Thee, O Lord, for Thou art good, and Thy mercy endureth forever. Amen.

✠

We thank Thee, Lord God, Heavenly Father, through Jesus Christ, our Lord, for all Thy benefits, who livest and reignest forever and ever. Amen.

✠

Lord God, gracious and merciful, we acknowledge Thy bountiful goodness toward us and give Thee thanks for our daily bread so richly provided by Thee. And we ask Thee to continue to bless us with the benedictions of Thy fatherly hands, through Jesus Christ, our Lord. Amen.

Selected Psalms

✠

Psalm 23

1. The Lord is my Shepherd; I shall not want.

2. He maketh me to lie in down in green pastures; He leadeth me beside the still waters.

3. He restoreth my soul; He leadeth me in the paths of righteousness for His name's sake.

4. Yea, though I walk through the valley of the shadow of death, I will fear no evil; for Thou art with me; Thy rod and Thy staff they comfort me.

5. Thou preparest a table before me in the presence of mine enemies; Thou anointest my head with oil; my cup runneth over.

6. Surely goodness and mercy shall follow me all the days of my life, and I will dwell in the house of the Lord forever.

✠

Psalm 32

1. Blessed is he whose transgression is forgiven, whose sin is covered.

2. Blessed is the man unto whom the Lord imputeth not iniquity and in whose spirit there is no guile.

3. When I kept silence, my bones waxed old through my roaring all the day long.

4. For day and night Thy hand was heavy upon me; my moisture is turned into the drought of summer. Selah.

5. I acknowledged my sin unto Thee, and mine iniquity have I not hid. I said, I will confess my transgressions unto the Lord; and Thou forgavest the iniquity of my sin. Selah.

6. For this shall every one that is godly pray unto Thee in a time when Thou mayest be found; surely in the floods of great waters they shall not come nigh unto him.

7. Thou art my Hiding Place; Thou shalt preserve me from trouble; Thou shalt compass me about with songs of deliverance. Selah.

8. I will instruct thee and teach thee in the way which thou shalt go; I will guide thee with Mine eye.

9. Be ye not as the horse or as the mule, which have no understanding; whose mouth must be held in with bit and bridle, lest they come near unto thee.

10. Many sorrows shall be to the wicked; but he that trusteth in the Lord, mercy shall compass him about.

11. Be glad in the Lord, and rejoice, ye righteous; and shout for joy, all ye that are upright in heart.

✠

Psalm 42

1. As the hart panteth after the water brooks, so panteth my soul after Thee, O God.

2. My soul thirsteth for God, for the living God; when shall I come and appear before God?

3. My tears have been my meat day and night, while they continually say unto me, Where is thy God?

4. When I remember these things, I pour out my soul in me; for I had gone with the multitude, I went with them to the house of God, with the voice of joy and praise, with a multitude that kept holyday.

5. Why art thou cast down, O my soul, and why art thou disquieted in me? Hope thou in God, for I shall yet praise Him for the help of His countenance.

6. O my God, my soul is cast down within me; therefore will I remember Thee from the land of Jordan, and of the Hermonites, from the hill Mizar.

7. Deep calleth unto deep at the noise of Thy waterspouts; all Thy waves and Thy billows are gone over me.

8. Yet the Lord will command His loving-kindness in the daytime, and in the night His song shall be with me, and my prayer unto the God of my life.

9. I will say unto God, my Rock, Why hast Thou forgotten me? Why go I mourning because of the oppression of the enemy?

10. As with a sword in my bones, mine enemies reproach me, while they say daily unto me, Where is thy God?

11. Why art thou cast down, O my soul, and why art thou disquieted within me? Hope thou in God; for I shall yet praise Him, who is the Health of my countenance and my God.

Psalm 46

1. God is our Refuge and Strength, a very present Help in trouble.

2. Therefore will not we fear, though the earth be removed, and though the mountains be carried into the midst of the sea;

3. Though the waters thereof roar and be troubled, though the mountains shake with the swelling thereof. Selah.

4. There is a river, the streams whereof shall make glad the city of God, the holy place of the tabernacles of the Most High.

5. God is in the midst of her; she shall not be moved; God shall help her, and that right early.

6. The heathen raged, the kingdoms were moved; He uttered His voice, the earth melted.

7. The Lord of Hosts is with us; the God of Jacob is our Refuge. Selah.

8. Come, behold the works of the Lord, what desolations He hath made in the earth.

9. He maketh wars to cease unto the end of the earth; He breaketh the bow, and cutteth the spear in sunder; He burneth the chariot in the fire.

10. Be still, and know that I am God; I will be exalted among the heathen, I will be exalted in the earth.

11. The Lord of Hosts is with us; the God of Jacob is our Refuge. Selah.

Psalm 51

PRAYER FOR REMISSION OF SINS AND FOR SANCTIFICATION

1. Have mercy upon me, O God, according to Thy loving-kindness; according unto the multitude of Thy tender mercies blot out my transgressions.

2. Wash me throughly, from mine iniquity, and cleanse me from my sin.

3. For I acknowledge my transgressions, and my sin is ever before me.

4. Against Thee, Thee only, have I sinned and done this evil in Thy sight, that Thou mightest be justified when Thou speakest, and be clear when Thou judgest.

5. Behold, I was shapen in iniquity, and in sin did my mother conceive me.

6. Behold, Thou desirest truth in the inward parts; and in the hidden part Thou shalt make me to know wisdom.

7. Purge me with hyssop, and I shall be clean; wash me, and I shall be whiter than snow.

8. Make me to hear joy and gladness, that the bones which Thou hast broken may rejoice.

9. Hide Thy face from my sins, and blot out all mine iniquities.

10. Create in me a clean heart, O God, and renew a right spirit within me.

11. Cast me not away from Thy presence, and take not Thy Holy Spirit from me.

12. Restore unto me the joy of Thy salvation, and uphold me with Thy free Spirit.

13. Then will I teach transgressors Thy ways, and sinners shall be converted unto Thee.

14. Deliver me from bloodguiltiness, O God, Thou God of my salvation, and my tongue shall sing aloud of Thy righteousness.

15. O Lord, open Thou my lips, and my mouth shall show forth Thy praise.

16. For Thou desirest not sacrifice; else would I give it; Thou delightest not in burnt offering.

17. The sacrifices of God are a broken spirit; a broken and a contrite heart, O God, Thou wilt not despise.

18. Do good in Thy good pleasure unto Zion; build Thou the walls of Jerusalem.

19. Then shalt Thou be pleased with the sacrifices of righteousness, with burnt offering and whole burnt offering; then shall they offer bullocks upon Thine altar.

✠

Psalm 63:1-8

1. O God, Thou art my God; early will I seek Thee; my soul thirsteth for Thee, my flesh longeth for Thee in a dry and thirsty land, where no water is;

2. To see Thy power and Thy glory, so as I have seen Thee in the sanctuary.

3. Because Thy loving-kindness is better than life, my lips shall praise Thee.

4. Thus will I bless Thee while I live; I will lift up my hands in Thy name.

5. My soul shall be satisfied as with marrow and fatness; and my mouth shall praise Thee with joyful lips;

6. When I remember Thee upon my bed and meditate on Thee in the night watches.

7. Because Thou hast been my Help, therefore in the shadow of Thy wings will I rejoice.

8. My soul followeth hard after Thee; Thy right hand upholdeth me.

✠

Psalm 121

1. I will lift up mine eyes unto the hills from whence cometh my help.

2. My help cometh from the Lord, which made heaven and earth.

3. He will not suffer thy foot to be moved; He that keepeth thee will not slumber.

4. Behold, He that keepeth Israel shall neither slumber nor sleep.

5. The Lord is thy Keeper; the Lord is thy Shade upon thy right hand.

6. The sun shall not smite thee by day nor the moon by night.

7. The Lord shall preserve thee from all evil; He shall preserve thy soul.

8. The Lord shall preserve thy going out and thy coming in from this time forth and even forevermore.

✠

Psalm 130

1. Out of the depths have I cried unto Thee, O Lord.

2. Lord, hear my voice; let Thine ears be attentive to the voice of my supplications.

3. If Thou, Lord, shouldest mark iniquities, O Lord, who shall stand?

4. But there is forgiveness with Thee, that Thou mayest be feared.

5. I wait for the Lord, my soul doth wait, and in His Word do I hope.

6. My soul waiteth for the Lord more than they that watch for the morning; I say, more than they that watch for the morning.

7. Let Israel hope in the Lord; for with the Lord there is mercy, and with Him is plenteous redemption.

8. And He shall redeem Israel from all his iniquities.

✠

Suggestions as to Other Psalms

Psalms of Praise and Thanksgiving: 103, 144—150

Psalms for Periods of Distress: 6, 28, 38, 77

Psalms for Times of Illness: 39, 65, 71, 90, 91

Psalms for Times of Spiritual Affliction: 73, 126

Psalms Pertaining to the Spreading of the Church: 87, 97

Psalms Asking Blessings upon Divine Worship:
    27, 100, 122

Psalms Exalting Christ and His Work: 2, 22, 45, 110

Psalms Asking for the Strengthening of Faith:
    34, 118, 139

Psalms for Those Discouraged: 25, 40, 86

Psalms for Convalescents: 84, 116, 138

The Nicene Creed

✠

I believe in one God, the Father Almighty, Maker of heaven and earth and of all things visible and invisible.

And in one Lord Jesus Christ, the only-begotten Son of God, begotten of His Father before all worlds, God of God, Light of Light, very God of very God, begotten, not made, being of one substance with the Father, by whom all things were made; who for us men and for our salvation came down from heaven and was incarnate by the Holy Ghost of the Virgin Mary, and was made man, and was crucified also for us under Pontius Pilate; He suffered and was buried; and the third day He rose again, according to the Scriptures; and ascended into heaven, and sitteth on the right hand of the Father; and He shall come again with glory to judge both the quick and the dead; whose kingdom shall have no end.

And I believe in the Holy Ghost, the Lord and Giver of Life, who proceedeth from the Father and the Son, who with the Father and the Son together is worshiped and glorified, who spake by the Prophets. And I believe one holy Christian and Apostolic Church. I acknowledge one Baptism for the remission of sins; and I look for the resurrection of the dead and the life of the world to come. Amen.

The Ten Commandments

✠

The First Commandment

Thou shalt have no other gods before Me.

What does this mean? Answer:

We should fear, love, and trust in God above all things.

The Second Commandment

Thou shalt not take the name of the Lord, thy God, in vain.

What does this mean? Answer:

We should fear and love God that we may not curse, swear, use witchcraft, lie, or deceive by His name, but call upon it in every trouble, pray, praise, and give thanks.

The Third Commandment

Thou shalt sanctify the holy day.

What does this mean? Answer:

We should fear and love God that we may not despise preaching and His Word, but hold it sacred and gladly hear and learn it.

The Fourth Commandment

Thou shalt honor thy father and thy mother that it may be well with thee and thou mayest live long on the earth.

What does this mean? Answer:

We should fear and love God that we may not despise our parents and masters, nor provoke them to anger, but give them honor, serve and obey them, and hold them in love and esteem.

The Fifth Commandment

Thou shalt not kill.

What does this mean? Answer:

We should fear and love God that we may not hurt nor harm our neighbor in his body, but help and befriend him in every bodily need.

The Sixth Commandment

Thou shalt not commit adultery.

What does this mean? Answer:

We should fear and love God that we may lead a chaste and decent life in word and deed, and each love and honor his spouse.

The Seventh Commandment

Thou shalt not steal.

What does this mean? Answer:

We should fear and love God that we may not take our neighbor's money or goods, nor get them by false ware or dealing, but help him to improve and protect his property and business.

The Eighth Commandment

Thou shalt not bear false witness against thy neighbor.

What does this mean? Answer:

We should fear and love God that we may not deceitfully belie, betray, slander, nor defame our neighbor, but defend him, speak well of him, and put the best construction on everything.

The Ninth Commandment

Thou shalt not covet thy neighbor's house.

What does this mean? Answer:

We should fear and love God that we may not craftily seek to get our neighbor's inheritance or house, nor obtain it by a show of right, but help and be of service to him in keeping it.

The Tenth Commandment

Thou shalt not covet thy neighbor's wife, nor his manservant, nor his maidservant, nor his cattle, nor anything that is thy neighbor's.

What does this mean? Answer:

We should fear and love God that we may not estrange, force, or entice away from our neighbor his wife, servants, or cattle, but urge them to stay and do their duty.

What does God say of all these Commandments? Answer:

He says thus: I, the Lord, thy God, am a jealous God, visiting the iniquity of the fathers upon the children unto the third and fourth generation of them that hate Me, and showing mercy unto thousands of them that love Me and keep My Commandments.

What does this mean? Answer:

God threatens to punish all that transgress these Commandments. Therefore we should fear His wrath and not act contrary to them. But He promises grace and every blessing to all that keep these Commandments. Therefore we should also love and trust in Him and willingly do according to His Commandments.

The Creed

✠

The First Article

OF CREATION

I believe in God the Father Almighty, Maker of heaven and earth.

What does this mean? Answer:

I believe that God has made me and all creatures; that He has given me my body and soul, eyes, ears, and all my members, my reason and all my senses, and still preserves them; also clothing and shoes, meat and drink, house and home, wife and children, fields, cattle, and all my goods; that He richly and daily provides me with all that I need to support this body and life; that He defends me against all danger and guards and protects me from all evil; and all this purely out of fatherly, divine goodness and mercy, without any merit or worthiness in me; for all which it is my duty to thank and praise, to serve and obey Him. This is most certainly true.

The Second Article

OF REDEMPTION

And in Jesus Christ, His only Son, our Lord, who was conceived by the Holy Ghost, born of the Virgin Mary, suffered under Pontius Pilate, was crucified, dead, and buried; He descended into hell; the third day He rose again from the dead; He ascended into heaven, and sitteth on the right hand of God the Father Almighty, from thence He shall come to judge the quick and the dead.

What does this mean? Answer:

I believe that Jesus Christ, true God, begotten of the Father from eternity, and also true man, born of the Virgin Mary, is my Lord, who has redeemed me, a lost and condemned creature, purchased and won me from all sins, from death, and from the power of the devil; not with gold or silver, but with His holy, precious blood and with His innocent suffering and death, that I may be His own and live under Him in His kingdom and serve Him in everlasting righteousness, innocence, and blessedness, even as He is risen from the dead, lives and reigns to all eternity. This is most certainly true.

The Third Article

OF SANCTIFICATION

I believe in the Holy Ghost; the holy Christian Church, the communion of saints; the forgiveness of sins; the resurrection of the body; and the life everlasting. Amen.

What does this mean? Answer:

I believe that I cannot by my own reason or strength believe in Jesus Christ, my Lord, or come to Him; but the Holy Ghost has called me by the Gospel, enlightened me with His gifts, sanctified and kept me in the true faith; even as He calls, gathers, enlightens, and sanctifies the whole Christian Church on earth and keeps it with Jesus Christ in the one true faith; in which Christian Church He daily and richly forgives all sins to me and all believers, and will at the Last Day raise up me and all the dead, and give unto me and all believers in Christ eternal life. This is most certainly true.

The Lord's Prayer

✠

Our Father who art in heaven.

What does this mean? Answer:

God would by these words tenderly invite us to
believe that He is our true Father and that we are
His true children, so that we may with all boldness
and confidence ask Him as dear children ask their
dear father.

The First Petition

Hallowed be Thy name.

What does this mean? Answer:

God's name is indeed holy in itself; but we pray
in this petition that it may be holy among us also.

How is this done? Answer:

When the Word of God is taught in its truth and
purity and we, as the children of God, also lead a
holy life according to it. This grant us, dear Father
in heaven. But he that teaches and lives otherwise
than God's Word teaches, profanes the name of God
among us. From this preserve us, Heavenly Father.

The Second Petition

Thy kingdom come.

How is this done? Answer:

The kingdom of God comes indeed without our prayer, of itself; but we pray in this petition that it may come unto us also.

How is this done? Answer:

When our heavenly Father gives us His Holy Spirit, so that by His grace we believe His holy Word and lead a godly life, here in time and hereafter in eternity.

The Third Petition

Thy will be done on earth as it is in heaven.

What does this mean? Answer:

The good and gracious will of God is done indeed without our prayer; but we pray in this petition that it may be done among us also.

How is this done? Answer:

When God breaks and hinders every evil counsel and will which would not let us hallow God's name nor let His kingdom come, such as the will of the devil, the world, and our flesh; but strengthens and preserves us steadfast in His Word and faith unto our end. This is His gracious and good will.

The Fourth Petition

Give us this day our daily bread.

What does this mean? Answer:

God gives daily bread indeed without our prayer, also to all the wicked; but we pray in this petition that He would lead us to know it and to receive our daily bread with thanksgiving.

What is meant by daily bread? Answer:

Everything that belongs to the support and wants of the body, such as food, drink, clothing, shoes, house, home, field, cattle, money, goods, a pious spouse, pious children, pious servants, pious and faithful rulers, good government, good weather, peace, health, discipline, honor, good friends, faithful neighbors, and the like.

The Fifth Petition

And forgive us our trespasses, as we forgive those who trespass against us.

What does this mean? Answer:

We pray in this petition that our Father in heaven would not look upon our sins, nor on their account deny our prayer; for we are worthy of none of the things for which we pray, neither have we deserved them; but that He would grant them all to us by grace; for we daily sin much and indeed deserve nothing but punishment. So will we also heartily forgive and readily do good to those who sin against us.

The Sixth Petition

And lead us not into temptation.

What does this mean? Answer:

God indeed tempts no one; but we pray in this petition that God would guard and keep us, so that the devil, the world, and our flesh may not deceive us nor seduce us into misbelief, despair, and other great shame and vice; and though we be assailed by them, that still we may finally overcome and obtain the victory.

The Seventh Petition

But deliver us from evil.

What does this mean? Answer:

We pray in this petition, as the sum of all, that our Father in heaven would deliver us from every evil of body and soul, property and honor, and finally, when our last hour has come, grant us a blessed end and graciously take us from this vale of tears to Himself in heaven.

Amen.

What does this mean? Answer:

That I should be certain that these petitions are acceptable to our Father in heaven and are heard by Him; for He Himself has commanded us so to pray, and has promised to hear us. Amen, Amen, that is, Yea, yea, it shall be so.

The Sacrament of Holy Baptism

✠

First

What is Baptism? Answer:

Baptism is not simple water only, but it is the water comprehended in God's command and connected with God's word.

Which is that word of God? Answer:

Christ, our Lord, says in the last chapter of Matthew: Go ye and teach all nations, baptizing them in the name of the Father and of the Son and of the Holy Ghost.

Secondly

What does Baptism give or profit? Answer:

It works forgiveness of sins, delivers from death and the devil, and gives eternal salvation to all who believe this, as the words and promises of God declare.

Which are such words and promises of God? Answer:

Christ, our Lord, says in the last chapter of Mark: He that believeth and is baptized shall be saved; but he that believeth not shall be damned.

Thirdly

How can water do such great things? Answer:

It is not the water indeed that does them, but the word of God which is in and with the water, and faith, which trusts such word of God in the water. For without the word of God the water is simple water and no Baptism. But with the word of God it is a Baptism, that is, a gracious water of life and a washing of regeneration in the Holy Ghost, as St. Paul says, Titus, chapter third:

By the washing of regeneration, and renewing of the Holy Ghost, which He shed on us abundantly through Jesus Christ, our Savior, that, being justified by His grace, we should be made heirs according to the hope of eternal life. This is a faithful saying.

Fourthly

What does such baptizing with water signify? Answer:

It signifies that the Old Adam in us should, by daily contrition and repentance, be drowned and die with all sins and evil lusts and, again, a new man daily come forth and arise, who shall live before God in righteousness and purity forever.

Where is this written? Answer:

St. Paul writes, Romans, chapter sixth: We are buried with Christ by Baptism into death, that, like as He was raised up from the dead by the glory of the Father, even so we also should walk in newness of life.

The Office of the Keys

✠

What is the Office of the Keys? Answer:

It is the peculiar church power which Christ has given to His Church on earth to forgive the sins of penitent sinners, but to retain the sins of the impenitent as long as they do not repent.

Where is this written? Answer:

Thus writes the holy Evangelist John, chapter twentieth:

The Lord Jesus breathed on His disciples and saith unto them, Receive ye the Holy Ghost. Whosoever sins ye remit, they are remitted unto them; and whosoever sins ye retain, they are retained.

What do you believe according to these words? Answer:

I believe that, when the called ministers of Christ deal with us by His divine command, especially when they exclude manifest and impenitent sinners from the Christian congregation, and, again, when they absolve those who repent of their sins and are willing to amend, this is as valid and certain, in heaven also, as if Christ, our dear Lord, dealt with us Himself.

How the Unlearned Should be Taught to Confess

What is Confession? Answer:

Confession embraces two parts. One is that we confess our sins; the other, that we receive absolution, or forgiveness, from the pastor, as from God Himself, and in no wise doubt, but firmly believe, that by it our sins are forgiven before God in heaven.

What sins should we confess? Answer:

Before God we should plead guilty of all sins, even of those which we do not know, as we do in the Lord's Prayer; but before the pastor we should confess those sins only which we know and feel in our hearts.

Which are these? Answer:

Here consider your station according to the Ten Commandments, whether you are a father, mother, son, daughter, master, mistress, servant; whether you have been disobedient, unfaithful, slothful; whether you have grieved any person by word or deed; whether you have stolen, neglected, or wasted aught, or done other injury.

The Sacrament of the Altar

✠

What is the Sacrament of the Altar? Answer:

It is the true body and blood of our Lord Jesus Christ under the bread and wine, for us Christians to eat and to drink, instituted by Christ Himself.

Where is this written? Answer:

The holy Evangelists Matthew, Mark, Luke, and St. Paul write thus:

Our Lord Jesus Christ, the same night in which He was betrayed, took bread; and when He had given thanks, He brake it and gave it to His disciples, saying, Take, eat; this is My body, which is given for you. This do in remembrance of Me.

After the same manner also He took the cup when He had supped, and when He had given thanks, He gave it to them, saying, Drink ye all of it; this cup is the new testament in My blood, which is shed for you for the remission of sins. This do, as oft as ye drink it, in remembrance of Me.

What is the benefit of such eating and drinking? Answer:

That is shown us by these words, "Given, and shed for you for the remission of sins"; namely, that in the Sacrament forgiveness of sins, life, and salvation are given us through these words. For where there is forgiveness of sins, there is also life and salvation.

How can bodily eating and drinking do such
great things? Answer:

It is not the eating and drinking, indeed, that does
them, but the words here written, "Given and shed
for you for the remission of sins"; which words,
besides the bodily eating and drinking, are the chief
thing in the Sacrament; and he that believes these
words has what they say and express, namely, the
forgiveness of sins.

Who, then, receives such Sacrament worthily? Answer:

Fasting and bodily preparation are indeed a fine
outward training; but he is truly worthy and well
prepared who has faith in these words, "Given and
shed for you for the remission of sins." But he that
does not believe these words, or doubts, is unworthy
and unprepared; for the words "for you" require all
hearts to believe.

Christian Questions with Their Answers

✠

Usually printed as a part of the Small Catechism of Dr. Martin Luther. — Drawn up by him for those who intend to go to the Sacrament

After Confession and instruction in the Ten Commandments, the Creed, the Lord's Prayer, and the Sacraments of Baptism and the Holy Supper, the pastor may ask, or one may ask himself:

1. Do you believe that you are a sinner?
   Yes, I believe it; I am a sinner.

2. How do you know this?
   From the Ten Commandments; these I have not kept.

3. Are you also sorry for your sins?
   Yes, I am sorry that I have sinned against God.

4. What have you deserved of God by your sins?
   His wrath and displeasure, temporal death, and eternal damnation. Rom. 6:21, 23.

5. Do you also hope to be saved?
   Yes, such is my hope.

6. In whom, then, do you trust?
   In my dear Lord Jesus Christ.

7. Who is Christ?
   The Son of God, true God and man.

8. How many Gods are there?
   Only one; but there are three Persons, Father, Son, and Holy Ghost.

9. What, then, has Christ done for you that you trust in Him?
   He died for me and shed His blood for me on the Cross for the forgiveness of sins.

10. Did the Father also die for you?
    He did not; for the Father is God only, the Holy Ghost likewise; but the Son is true God and true man; He died for me and shed His blood for me.

11. How do you know this?
    From the holy Gospel and from the words of the Sacrament, and by His body and blood given me as a pledge in the Sacrament.

12. How do those words read?
    Our Lord Jesus Christ, the same night in which He was betrayed, took bread; and when He had given thanks, He brake it and gave it to His disciples, saying, Take, eat; this is My body, which is given for you. This do in remembrance of Me.
    After the same manner also He took the cup when He had supped, and when He had given thanks, He gave it to them, saying, Drink ye all of it; this cup is the new testament in My blood, which is shed for you for the remission of sins. This do, as oft as ye drink it, in remembrance of Me.

13. You believe, then, that the true body and blood of Christ are in the Sacrament
    Yes, I believe it.

14. What induces you to believe this?

    The word of Christ, Take, eat, this is My body;
    Drink ye all of it, this is My blood.

15. What ought we to do when we eat His body
    and drink His blood, and thus receive the pledge?

    We ought to remember and proclaim His death
    and the shedding of His blood, as He taught us:
    This do, as oft as ye drink it, in remembrance
    of Me.

16. Why ought we to remember and proclaim His
    death?

    That we may learn to believe that no creature
    could make satisfaction for our sins but Christ,
    true God and man; and that we may learn to
    look with terror at our sins, and to regard them
    as great indeed, and to find joy and comfort in
    Him alone, and thus be saved through such faith.

17. What was it that moved Him to die and make
    satisfaction for your sins?

    His great love to His Father and to me and other
    sinners, as it is written in John 14; Romans 5;
    Galatians 2; Ephesians 5.

18. Finally, why do you wish to go to the Sacra-
    ment?

    That I may learn to believe that Christ died for
    my sin out of great love, as before said; and that
    I may also learn of Him to love God and my
    neighbor.

19. What should admonish and incite a Christian
    to receive the Sacrament frequently?

In respect to God, both the command and the promise of Christ the Lord should move him; and in respect to himself, the trouble that lies heavy on him, on account of which such command, encouragement, and promise are given.

20. But what shall a person do if he be not sensible of such trouble and feel no hunger and thirst for the Sacrament

To such a person no better advice can be given than that, in the first place, he put his hand into his bosom and feel whether he still have flesh and blood, and that he by all means believe what the Scriptures say of it, in Galatians 5 and Romans 7.

Secondly, that he look around to see whether he is still in the world, and keep in mind that there will be no lack of sin and trouble, as the Scriptures say in John 15 and 16; 1 John 2 and 5.

Thirdly, he will certainly have the devil also about him, who with his lying and murdering, day and night, will let him have no peace within or without, as the Scriptures picture him in John 8 and 16; 1 Peter 5; Ephesians 6; 2 Timothy 2.

NOTE

These questions and answers are no child's play, but are drawn up with great earnestness of purpose by the venerable and pious Dr. Luther for both young and old. Let each one take heed and likewise consider it a serious matter; for St. Paul writes to the Galatians, chapter sixth: "Be not deceived; God is not mocked."

TABLE OF CONTENTS

Preface   5

The Lord's Prayer   7

Prayers for Mornings and Evenings
    First Set   10
    Second Set   24
    Third Set   38
    Fourth Set   52
    A General Morning Prayer   66
    A General Evening Prayer   67

Prayers for Certain Times and Seasons
    Advent   70
    Christmas Eve   71
    Christmas Day   72
    New Year's Eve   73
    New Year's Day   74
    Epiphany   75
    Lent   76
    Ash Wednesday   77
    Palm Sunday   78

        HOLY WEEK

    Monday   79
    Tuesday   80
    Wednesday   81
    Maundy Thursday   82
    Good Friday   84
    Saturday   85
    Early Easter Morning   87
    Easter   87

Ascension   89
Pentecost   90
Pentecost — For the Church   91
Trinity Sunday   92
Reformation Sunday   93
Thanksgiving Day   94
Day of Humiliation and Prayer   95
A Confession of Sins   96
Prayer for College Students   97
For Our Colleges and Seminaries   98
For the Christian Day School   99
For My Sunday School   101
For the Church at Large   102
For Missions at Home   103
For Missions Abroad   104
For the Ministers of the Word   105
For the Teachers of the Church   106
For the Congregation   107
Before Confession and Absolution   108
Before Holy Communion (Prayer at Home)   109
Before Communion (At Church)   110
After Holy Communion   111
On the Day of Confirmation of a Child   112
In Memory of Confirmation   113
Concerning Holy Baptism   114

Prayers Pertaining to National Affairs
For Peace   116
On Independence Day   117
On Independence Day   118

On Memorial Day 119
On Veterans' Day 120
On Labor Day 121
In Days of Unemployment 122
For Lawmaking Bodies 123
For the Government 124
For Fields and Crops 125
In a Storm 126
At the Time of an Epidemic 127
At the Threat of War (In Our Own Nation) 128
At the Outbreak of War 129
In a National Crisis 130
In a National Calamity 131

Prayers for Various Occasions in Individual and Family Life

On the Day of a Wedding Anniversary 134
Of Husband and Wife 135
Of a Woman with Child 136
At the Birth of a Child 137
At the Baptism of a Child 138
At the Baptism of a Child 139
Of a Sponsor 140
Of Parents 140
Of Children 142
For an Erring Child 143
Upon Occupying a New Home 144
For the Home 145
For the Home 146
For Those Away from Home 147
While Away from Home 148

215

For a Member of the Family in Danger 149
In Times of Illness in the Family 150
Of One Who Is Ill 151
Of One Who Is Ill 152
Of One Who Is Ill 153
Of One Who Is Ill 153
Before an Operation 154
After an Operation 155
Of a Convalescent 156
Of a Convalescent 157
At the Approach of Death 158
After a Death 159
Of Mourners 160
Of a Mourner 161
On One's Birthday 162
Of Those Engaged 163
Of One in Love 164
Of a Young Person 165
Of a Businessman 166
In Business Reverses 167
During Hard Times 168
In Days of Personal Unemployment 169
In Behalf of the Unemployed 170
For an Aviator 171
A Soldier's Prayer 172
A Soldier's Prayer 173
Of a Student of Theology (For Faithfulness
     and Diligence) 175
Of a Student of Theology (For Sincerity) 176
For Stronger Faith 177

For a Sanctified Life 178
Prayers at Table 180
    Before the Meal 180
    After the Meal 181
Selected Psalms 182
The Nicene Creed 190
The Ten Commandments 191
The Creed 195
The Lord's Prayer 198
The Sacrament of Holy Baptism 202
The Office of the Keys 204
The Sacrament of the Altar 206
Christian Questions with Their Answers 208